Exotic Cuisines

Exotic **C**uisines

**Over 250 delicious recipes
from 20 of the most exciting cuisines
of the world**

Edited by Diana Vowles

THE
APPLE
PRESS

(Apple Press)

A QUINTET BOOK

Published by the Apple Press
6 Blundell Street
London N7 9BH

ISBN 1–85076–516–2

This book was designed and produced by
Quintet Publishing Limited
6 Blundell Street
London N7 9BH

Creative Director: Richard Dewing
Designer: Isobel Gillan
Project Editor: Anna Briffa
Editor: Diana Vowles
Illustrator: Rowan Clifford

Typeset in Great Britain by
Central Southern Typesetters, Eastbourne
Manufactured in Hong Kong by Regent Publishing Services Limited
Printed in China by Leefung-Asco Printers Limited

The material in this publication previously appeared in:
*Low Fat Indian Cooking, The Complete Indian Cookbook, Mexican Cooking, Russian
Regional Recipes, Lebanese Cooking, Greek Meze Cooking, Creole Cooking, Nuevo Cubano
Cooking, Spanish Cooking, Cajun Cooking, Vietnamese Cooking, Recipes from a Polish
Kitchen, The Fresh Pasta Cookbook, Classic Chinese and Oriental Cooking, The Complete
Chinese Cookbook, Step by Step Japanese Cooking*

Contents

Introduction

Once upon a time, the meals found in British households were composed of a limited number of ingredients. The lamb might have come from New Zealand and fruit such as bananas and pineapples certainly weren't found in British orchards, but most of the produce was home grown. Reassuringly British veg (always two) accompanied meat that was roasted, fried or grilled in its natural state, a stranger to marinades, sauces and seasonings save perhaps a dusting of salt and pepper.

It wasn't always thus. In the days before there was refrigeration, herbs and seasonings were used extensively to try to preserve the meat for longer (and to disguise the aroma when the attempt failed). Old cookery books prove that British food was once rich, varied and inventive. So what happened? Perhaps it was the two world wars, the first of which removed the domestic staff from the majority of British households and left the housewife suddenly in charge of meals which would once have been the responsibility of the professional cook. The second introduced strict food rationing and an austerity diet where hedonism was an ounce of butter per week. Maybe it was the arrival of the fridge in most homes, which meant that meat could safely be kept without spicing. Whatever the reason, the British diet suffered, for the native ingredients of which we were once so proud began to lose their quality as factory farming got under way and produce that could once have held its own naked and unadorned now badly needed a helping hand with the spice jar.

While London and other major cities were more cosmopolitan in their outlook, it was not until the Sixties that exotica such as green peppers and courgettes made their appearance in provincial towns. They were the thin end of the wedge. As package holidays took off and Brits began to sample foreign food as a yearly treat, a whole new world of gastronomy presented itself. Dishes were discovered to contain wine, fresh herbs, strange flavours. People who were afraid of garlic ate it in Majorca, Paris, Rome and Benidorm and lived. Was there any reason why we couldn't dine like this at home?

Just as we were adjusting to the idea of continental food, Indian restaurants began popping up like mushrooms all over the land. As a nation, we fell upon the idea of curry and poppadoms as an alternative to fish and chips with unbridled enthusiasm. Chinese takeaways became part of daily life, too. And it didn't stop there – supermarkets rose to the challenge of our new-found cosmopolitanism and before long star fruit, mangoes and papayas shouldered Cox's orange pippins and hot pepper, soya and hoisin sauces stood in neat ranks on the shelves alongside good old Branston pickle.

Now we can choose our meals from all over the world, but it's not always easy to know how to use this bewildering array of produce. We eat at ethnic restaurants and return home wondering how we can reproduce a particularly delicious dish in our own kitchens. Now, more than ever, we need the aid of cookery books, for this is not the kind of cooking that we could have learnt from our mothers.

This book has been compiled to trawl a range of dishes from our global village. Within it you will find classics such as Chicken Kiev, Peking Duck and Gazpacho, along with a variety of probably unfamiliar dishes which are nevertheless easy to master. It celebrates the hot, spicy food of Mexico, the endlessly inventive cuisine of China, the delicate flavours of Vietnam. It is also a testament to the way in which national cuisines are inextricably linked with history – for example, in the food of the Caribbean there are to be found Indian, Chinese, French, British and African influences; many Spanish dishes bear the imprint of the Moorish invaders who ruled the country for three centuries; and Lebanese cuisine encompasses ingredients and styles drawn from France, Syria, Iraq and Italy.

Many exotic ingredients are now a familiar sight – any self-respecting supermarket stocks the ground cumin, cardomom, coriander, turmeric and chilli powder essential to Indian food. However, some of the recipes contained in this book do use more uncommon ingredients which require a bit of explanation.

SPECIAL INGREDIENTS

Bamboo shoots   There are several kinds of canned bamboo shoots available in the West. Try to obtain the Winter ones, which are particularly tender and flavoursome. Once the can has been opened the shoots may be kept in the refrigerator, covered with water, for several days. Bamboo shoots sold as braised should be eaten cold without any further cooking.

Banh Pho   These are short, flat Vietnamese rice stick noodles about 4 mm/⅛ in wide. They cook in minutes when placed in boiling water or soup and should not be overdone.

Banh Trang   This is round, semi-transparent rice paper used as a wrapping for Vietnamese spring rolls and grilled meats. The dough is made from finely ground rice, water and salt, with tapioca flour as a binding agent.

Bean curd (tofu)   Bean curd is made from soaked yellow soya beans ground with water. It has a mild, slightly nutty flavour and is a good source of vegetable protein. Sold in blocks in supermarkets, health shops and Oriental groceries, it can be kept in the refrigerator for a few days if covered with water. Dried bean curd skin is sold either in thick sticks or thin sheets. It should be soaked in cold water overnight or in warm water for an hour before use.

Bean sauce   There are two types of bean sauce, black and yellow. The former is very salty, while the latter has a sweet flavour. Bean sauce is made from beans, flour and salt. Once the container is opened it must be stored in the refrigerator, where it can be kept for months.

Bean sprouts   Yellow soya bean sprouts are available from Chinese groceries, but the most commonly used type are mung bean sprouts, which are widely available. Do not use canned bean sprouts, as the attractive crunchy texture is lost. Bean sprouts will keep for two or three days in the refrigerator.

Chinese dried mushrooms   There are two main types of Chinese mushrooms: those that grow on trees, known as fragrant or winter mushrooms, and those grown on straw, called straw mushrooms. Fragrant mushrooms are sold dried and should be soaked in warm water for 20–30 minutes then squeezed dry before use. The hard stalks should be discarded. Straw mushrooms, available in cans, have a very different flavour and texture. Western mushrooms can be used as a substitute.

Coconut milk   Coconut milk is frequently used in Oriental, Asian and Caribbean dishes. It is not the liquid contained in the coconut itself. To make it, combine the grated flesh of a coconut with 500 ml/18 fl oz very hot water. Pass the liquid through a sieve, squeezing the pulp to extract all the liquid, called thick coconut milk or coconut cream. If the recipe calls for thin coconut milk, add a further 500 ml/18 fl oz water to the same pulp and repeat the process. A quick method of making coconut milk is to blend 75 g/3 oz creamed coconut with 500 ml/18 fl oz hot water. Creamed coconut is available from supermarkets and Asian grocers in 200 g/7 oz slabs.

Dried shrimp   These small shrimp are sold cleaned, shelled and whole. They give a salty, savoury seasoning to dishes.

Five spice powder   This blend of anise, fennel, cloves, cinnamon and pepper is a staple seasoning in Chinese cookery. It is highly flavoured, so use sparingly.

Ghee   Clarified butter, made by heating the butter over a low heat until all the white residue turns golden and settles at the bottom. Strain, pour into an airtight bottle and store in a cool place. Alternatively, ghee can be bought in tins from Asian grocers and some general supermarkets. It is useful in cooking as it can be heated to a high temperature without burning.

Ginger   See root ginger.

Hoisin sauce   A sauce made from soya beans, sugar, flour, vinegar, salt, garlic, chilli and sesame seeds which is frequently used in Chinese cookery. It is available in Chinese groceries and many supermarkets.

Mirin Mirin, a sweet cooking wine with a very low alcohol content, is an essential item in Japanese kitchens. It gives a distinctive mild sweetness to simmering liquids, glazes and dipping sauces. It is to be found in Japanese food shops and some health shops. If you are unable to obtain it, simply substitute 1 tsp sugar per 1 tbsp mirin.

Nuoc Mam A pungent fish sauce used extensively in South-East Asian cooking. It is made by layering fish and salt into large barrels and leaving the fish to ferment for three months. The accumulated liquid is then drawn off and bottled.

Oyster sauce A thick sauce made from oysters and soya beans, used in Chinese cooking. It is available in Chinese groceries and supermarkets. Stored in the refrigerator, it will keep indefinitely.

Pigeon peas These small round peas are also known as gunga or gungo peas, congo peas, arhar dah and channa peas. They are obtainable in most Asian and West Indian grocers. They are very popular in the West Indies and generally are used for the classic dish of rice and peas, though some of the Caribbean countries favour red kidney beans instead.

Plantain This is a member of the banana family, but it is not for eating raw. The flesh can be yellow, ivory or pink. Plantains are sold both green (in which case they are usually boiled) and ripe, when they are yellow and brown. If the recipe calls for ripe plantains and you can only find green, place them in the oven at 150°C/300°F/Gas Mark 2 until the skin turns black and begins to split.

Ponzu sauce A sauce used in a variety of Japanese dishes. It is made by combining lemon juice, mirin, sake, soy sauce, seaweed and bonito flakes and can be bought ready-made from Japanese food shops.

Rice wine A Chinese wine made from glutinous rice, also known as Shaoxing wine. Sake or medium or dry sherry can be substituted.

Root ginger Fresh root ginger is widely used all over the world. It is easily available, particularly in shops selling Oriental, Asian, African and West Indian produce. Dried or stem ginger is not a substitute. Peel off the hard brown skin with a knife before chopping or grating. To obtain ginger juice, squeeze freshly grated ginger.

Sake A Japanese wine made from fermented rice. If it is unobtainable, use medium or dry sherry instead.

Sesame seed oil In China, this is used as a garnish rather than for cooking. It is widely available in Chinese groceries and supermarkets.

Seven-spice pepper Used in Japanese cooking, this is a mixture of chilli pepper, black pepper, dried orange peel, sesame seeds, poppy seeds, slivers of nori seaweed and hemp seeds. The proportions of the ingredients are variable. It is available in Japanese food shops.

Sichuan peppercorns These reddish-brown peppercorns are much stronger than the black and white peppercorns used in the West. They are usually sold in plastic bags.

Tamarind A fruit sold squashed into bricks. Its tart, citric flavour is not unlike lemon, which can be used as a substitute. To make tamarind juice, soak 75 g/3 oz tamarind in 250 ml/8 fl oz hot water for about 30 minutes. Squeeze the pulp to extract all the juice, strain and use as required.

Wasabi This is the Japanese equivalent of horseradish and is the grated root of a riverside plant that is native to Japan. It is sold in Japanese groceries ready made in tubes and in powder form, to be mixed with a little water to form a paste. It is usually used as an accompaniment to raw fish dishes.

Water chestnuts These do not in fact belong to the chestnut family – they are a root vegetable. They are available both fresh and in cans; the fresh ones have a much better flavour and texture. They will keep for about a month in the refrigerator.

Wood ears Dried tree fungus, also known as cloud ears. Soak in warm water for 20 minutes, discard hard stems and rinse before use. They have a crunchy texture and a mild, subtle flavour.

Yuca Also called cassava, this is a starchy tuber with a bark-like skin. It is used extensively in Cuban and Caribbean cooking. If it is unobtainable, substitute potatoes.

Soups

Soups feature in cuisines all over the world. They may be clear, delicate and elegant, hot, spicy and enlivening or thick and filling, a meal in themselves. In this chapter you'll find a soup to suit every occasion.

CHINESE

GOOD STOCK

SERVES 12

1.5–1.75 kg/3–4 lb chicken or duck carcass or spareribs	2 litres/3¼ pt water 3–4 slices root ginger

◆ Remove the breast meat and the legs from the chicken. Boil the remaining carcass of the chicken in 1.75 litres/3 pt water for 20 minutes. Remove from the heat and add the remaining water. (The adding of the cold water causes the fat and impurities to cling together, making them easier to remove.) Skim the surface of all scum which rises to the top. Add the ginger and continue to simmer gently for about 1 hour.

◆ Remove the chicken carcass from the stock. Mince the leg meat and the breast meat separately. Add the leg meat to the stock. Simmer for 10 minutes, then add the breast meat and simmer for about 5 minutes. Strain the stock through a fine sieve or muslin.

CHINESE

BEANSPROUT SOUP

SERVES 4–6

225 g/8 oz fresh beansprouts	2 tsp salt
1 small sweet red pepper, cored and seeded	600 ml/1 pt water
30 ml/2 tbsp oil	1 spring onion, finely chopped, to garnish

◆ Wash the beansprouts in cold water, discarding the husks and other bits and pieces that float to the surface. It is not necessary to top and tail each sprout. Thinly shred the pepper.

◆ Heat a wok or large pot, add the oil and wait for it to smoke. Add the beansprouts and red pepper and stir a few times. Add the salt and water. When the soup starts to boil, garnish with finely chopped spring onion and serve hot.

NUEVO CUBANO

SPLIT-PEA SOUP WITH CHORIZO

The chorizo in this classic soup gives it a modern twist. It makes a spectacular lunch for company.

SERVES 4–6

675 g/1½ lb cured chorizo, casing removed and thinly sliced	1 litre/1¾ pt water
1 onion, chopped	½ tsp dried thyme
1 stick celery, finely chopped	1 bay leaf
2 cloves garlic, minced	3 carrots, halved lengthwise, and thinly sliced crosswise
450 g/1 lb split peas, picked over	salt and freshly ground black pepper
1 litre/1¾ pt chicken stock	croûtons, to garnish

◆ In a heavy-based saucepan over moderate heat, brown the chorizo, stirring constantly. Transfer with a slotted spoon to absorbent kitchen paper to drain, and pour off all but 1 tbsp fat. In the remaining fat, cook the onion, celery and garlic over moderately low heat, stirring until the celery is softened. Then add the split peas, stock, water, thyme and bay leaf, cover and simmer, stirring occasionally, for 1¼ hours.

◆ Stir in the carrots and simmer, covered, until the carrots are tender, 30–35 minutes. Discard the bay leaf, add the cooked chorizo, season with salt and pepper, and serve with croûtons.

BEAN SOUP WITH PARSLEY, GARLIC AND CHILLI

SERVES 4

350 g/12 oz dried white kidney
    beans
4 cloves garlic, crushed
60 ml/4 tbsp olive oil

60 ml/4 tbsp tomato purée
2 tbsp finely chopped fresh parsley
25 g/1 oz fresh chillies
salt and pepper to taste

◆ Soak the kidney beans in double their volume of water overnight. Leave the pot near a low heat source such as a radiator or pilot light if you can.

◆ At least 90 minutes before you wish to serve the soup, drain the beans, cover them with more water and set them to boil over a low heat. Cook them for 40–60 minutes, until they are tender. If you are using them immediately, let them stand in their cooking water. Otherwise, drain and store covered in the fridge.

◆ Soften the garlic in the olive oil over a low heat. As it begins to colour, drain away as much of the oil as you can and set it aside.

◆ Add the cooked beans, the tomato purée, the parsley and no more than 300 ml/½ pt of water. Bring the mixture to the boil then lower the heat to simmer.

◆ As the soup is cooking, slice and seed the fresh chillies and stew them very gently in the garlic-flavoured olive oil until they are very soft. Pour the chilli oil into a small serving bowl.

◆ Take half the quantity of the bean soup and liquidize it. When the consistency is completely smooth, stir the two parts of the soup together thoroughly.

◆ Check the seasoning. The soup is now ready to serve.

WHITE BEAN AND YUCA VICHYSSOISE

Toss some leftover bits of chorizo, ham or flank steak into this concoction after it's puréed and you have a Nuevo version of Galician Bean Soup, so beloved by Cubans. This potage is a variation on the authentic dish, which contains turnip, collard or mustard greens and none of the gentle seasoning.

SERVES 4–6

10 ml/2 tsp plus 30 ml/2 tbsp olive oil, divided

4 tsp white wine

4 cloves garlic, crushed

25 g/1 oz butter or margarine

2 leeks, sliced and rinsed

2 sticks celery, sliced

2 × 500 g/19 oz tins cannellini (white kidney beans), drained and rinsed

450 g/1 lb yuca or potatoes, peeled and cut into 5 cm/2 in sections

900 ml/1½ pt chicken stock

2 tsp chopped fresh rosemary

2 tsp chopped fresh thyme leaves

2 tsp chopped fresh sage

2 bay leaves

salt and freshly ground white pepper to taste

2 tbsp snipped fresh chives, to garnish (optional)

◆ In a small pan, heat 2 tsp olive oil and the white wine. Add the garlic and sauté over a low flame for about 10 minutes.

◆ Meanwhile, heat the remaining olive oil and the butter in a large saucepan. Add the leeks and celery and sauté until wilted, about 10 minutes. Add the beans and yuca to the leeks with the chicken stock, herbs and bay leaves. Add the garlic mixture and simmer until the yuca is soft, about 30 minutes. Remove the bay leaves. Add salt and pepper to taste. Purée in a blender or food processor. Garnish with chives and serve.

YELLOW SQUASH AND POTATO SOUP

A smooth, thick broth is poured over bits of browned potato in this rich, yet inexpensive, soup. If you want to make ahead, refrigerate after puréeing, then reheat and add the cream just before serving.

SERVES 4

25 g/1 oz butter

100 g/4 oz onion, chopped

1 clove garlic, finely chopped

2 baking potatoes, cubed but not peeled

2–3 yellow courgettes, sliced

750 ml/1¼ pt chicken stock

pinch of cayenne pepper

pinch of freshly ground black pepper

1 tsp paprika

½ tsp thyme

½ tsp basil

175 ml/6 fl oz single cream

salt to taste

◆ In a frying pan over medium heat, melt the butter. Sauté the onion and garlic until wilted, about 5 minutes. Add the potatoes and sauté for 8–10 minutes. (You may need to add another 15 g/½ oz butter at this point.) Remove 100 g/4 oz potatoes and keep warm. Add the squash to the frying pan and sauté for about 3 minutes.

◆ In a saucepan, mix together the chicken stock and seasonings, then add the sautéed vegetables. Bring to the boil, then reduce the heat and simmer for about 40 minutes. Purée the soup in batches in a blender or food processor.

◆ Return the puréed soup to the saucepan and heat through. Add the cream and salt to taste and heat through but do not boil. Divide the reserved potatoes among serving bowls and ladle the soup over the potatoes.

CREAMY CHESTNUT SOUP

Chestnuts replace beans in the cooking of Galicia and they are used in the same way as potatoes are elsewhere in Europe. Here they make a delicious, creamy winter soup, delicately flavoured with a little cinnamon.

SERVES 4

450 g/1 lb unshelled chestnuts (or 350 g/12 oz peeled)	60 ml/4 tbsp olive oil
salt and freshly ground black pepper	30 ml/2 tbsp red-wine vinegar
1 thick slice bread	about 700 ml/1¼ pt light stock
	⅛ tsp cinnamon

◆ Slash the chestnut shells across the fat part of the nut, drop into a pan and cover with cold water with a little salt. Bring to the boil and cook for 20 minutes. Let them cool (but leave under water). When cool, peel the chestnuts, removing the brown skin too.

◆ Fry the bread in the oil then put it in a blender or food processor and purée with the vinegar. Reserve a handful of coarsely chopped nuts to add texture to the soup and add the rest to the blender, a little at a time, with some of the stock. Purée to a cream. Return the creamed soup to the pan, taste and season with salt and pepper. Flavour discreetly with the cinnamon. Add the chopped nuts, heat through and serve.

SWEETCORN AND ASPARAGUS SOUP

SERVES 4–6

175 g/6 oz white asparagus	1 tsp salt
1 egg white	100 g/4 oz sweetcorn
1 tbsp cornflour	1 spring onion, finely chopped, to
30 ml/2 tbsp water	garnish
600 ml/1 pt water	

◆ Cut the asparagus spears into small cubes. Beat the egg white lightly. Mix the cornflour with 2 tbsp water to make a smooth paste. Bring 600 ml/1 pt water to a rolling boil. Add the salt, sweetcorn and asparagus. When the water starts to boil again, add the cornflour and water mixture, stirring constantly. Add the egg white very slowly and stir. Serve hot, garnished with finely chopped spring onion.

Above: Red Gazpacho

RED GAZPACHO

If you like your soup thick rather than puréed, chop the vegetables by hand. While it takes a little longer to do it this way, another benefit is that you can serve the vegetables separately from the soup and let your family or guests spoon in the items they want. Tortilla chips make wonderful "crackers" for serving with gazpacho.

SERVES 4–6

450 ml/¾ pt tomato juice
30 ml/2 tbsp olive oil
¾ tsp chilli powder
¼ large onion, quartered and finely chopped
1 small cucumber, peeled, seeded and finely chopped

2 small sweet green peppers, seeded and finely chopped
3 medium to large tomátoes, finely chopped
2 large cloves garlic, crushed
salt and freshly ground black pepper to taste

◆ In a blender or food processor, combine the tomato juice, olive oil and chilli powder. Whirl until the liquid is well blended. Chill at this point if you do not want to serve the soup already mixed.

◆ In a large bowl, combine the tomato juice mixture with the chopped vegetables and crushed garlic. Chill until ready to serve. Season with salt and pepper just before serving.

VERMICELLI SOUP

If you make it thin, this is a soup. If you decrease the amount of stock, increase the quantities of the other ingredients, and add some minced meat, you have a dish which is more akin to spaghetti bolognese. Both versions are, of course, authentic. This is for the thinner version:

SERVES 6

100 g/4 oz vermicelli, broken up
15 g/½ oz lard
1–2 cloves garlic, finely chopped
1.5 litres/2½ pt beef stock
½ small onion, finely chopped

400 g/14 oz can tomatoes, chopped with their liquid
1 tsp dried oregano
salt and pepper

◆ Fry the vermicelli in the lard until it is golden – about 5 minutes. Stir constantly to avoid burning. Reduce the heat; add the garlic and fry for another 30 seconds to 1 minute to soften the garlic and precook it. Add the rest of the ingredients and bring to the boil. Simmer for 30 minutes, stirring occasionally.

CUCUMBER SOUP

SERVES 4–6

½ cucumber
50 g/2 oz black field mushrooms
600 ml/1 pt water

1½ tsp salt
5 ml/1 tsp sesame seed oil
1 spring onion, finely chopped

◆ Split the cucumber in half lengthwise, and thinly slice but do not peel. Wash and slice the mushrooms, but do not peel. Bring the water to the boil in a wok or large pot. Add the cucumber and mushroom slices and salt. Boil for about 1 minute. Add the sesame seed oil and finely chopped spring onion, stir and serve hot.

MEXICAN

GARLIC SOUP

Because the garlic is first fried then boiled in the soup, this does not taste anything like as overpowering as most people expect. In fact, it is a very delicate soup.

SERVES 4

10 cloves garlic	croûtons or well-browned toast
½ tsp flour	(optional)
25 g/1 oz butter	
1 litre/1¾ pt beef or chicken stock	**To garnish**
Tabasco sauce	2 tbsp crumbled cheese
salt and pepper	1 tbsp chopped parsley
4 eggs	

◆ Chop the garlic as finely as possible, then mash. Add the flour, and fry gently in butter. When it is translucent, add the stock; bring to the boil and simmer for 15 minutes. Strain through a fine-mesh sieve; season with Tabasco sauce, salt and pepper.

◆ Return to the heat. With the soup at a gentle boil, slip in the eggs and poach them. When they are firm, the soup is done. Serve over croûtons or toast; garnish with crumbled cheese and parsley.

VARIATIONS

Instead of serving the soup in the usual way, in a tureen, try this:
◆ Heat four individual serving bowls in the oven at about 120°C/250°F/Gas Mark ½. Pour the boiling soup into these, and add the egg *yolk* only. Leave to stand for a couple of minutes, preferably covered, and serve. The yolk will still be liquid, but this is quite normal in Mexico. Add the croûtons with the garnish, or omit them.
◆ Yet another variation calls for using a fried egg. Fry the egg lightly in olive oil, and slide on to the soup, "sunny-side up". The croûtons are useful here to support the egg.

CHINESE

CHINESE CABBAGE SOUP

SERVES 4–6

275 g/9 oz Chinese cabbage	2 tsp salt
3–4 dried Chinese mushrooms,	15 ml/1 tbsp rice wine or dry sherry
soaked in warm water for	900 ml/1½ pt water
30 minutes	5 ml/1 tsp sesame seed oil
30 ml/2 tbsp oil	

◆ Wash the cabbage and cut it into thin slices. Squeeze dry the soaked mushrooms. Discard the hard stalks and cut the mushrooms into small pieces. Reserve the water in which the mushrooms have been soaked for use later.
◆ Heat a wok or large pot until hot, add the oil and wait for it to smoke. Add the cabbage and mushrooms. Stir a few times and then add the salt, wine, water and the mushroom soaking water. Bring to the boil, add the sesame seed oil and serve.

CALDO TLALPENO

About the only constant things in Caldo Tlalpeno (Tlalpen-style soup) are chicken and avocado. Sometimes the soup is made with a chicken stock; sometimes with vegetable stock. Usually (but not invariably) it contains some kind of chilli pepper, though which sort of pepper varies widely. Gringo versions usually contain little or no garlic; Mexican versions may contain a whole head. This is a simple, authentic version.

SERVES 4

100 g/4 oz chicken (white meat)	45 ml/3 tbsp water
1 litre/1¾ pt chicken stock	salt to taste (½–1 tsp)
1–2 dried red chillies, deseeded and chopped	1 avocado
1–5 cloves garlic	coriander, to garnish (about half a handful)

◆ Slice the chicken into julienne strips. If the chicken is not cooked, bring the chicken stock to a boil; simmer the meat until it is cooked (less than 5 minutes). Otherwise, bring the stock and chicken to a simmering boil. Doubling the amount of chicken will not do any harm.

◆ Grind the chillies in a pestle and mortar with the garlic and water. Strain into the stock. Stir, simmer for a couple of minutes, and add salt to taste.

◆ Peel the avocado and slice into strips. Separate the slices carefully before dropping them into the soup, or they will stick together. They will sink for a few moments, then float to the surface. When they do, the soup is ready. Chop some coriander and float it on the surface for a garnish.

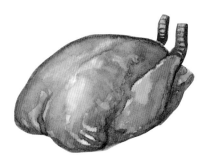

SHERRIED LOBSTER BISQUE

This is a rich, delectable soup. Monkfish is the best substitute for lobster, but any firm-fleshed fish, such as red snapper or cod, will do. Pair this soup with a green salad and some crusty bread and you have a memorable meal.

SERVES 4–6

40 g/1½ oz butter
10–12 sticks celery, chopped
1 onion, chopped
¼ tsp dried thyme
½ tsp chilli pepper flakes
1 tbsp slivers fresh lemon rind
20 g/¾ oz self-raising flour
250 ml/8 fl oz chicken stock
250 ml/8 fl oz milk

450 g/1 lb lobster meat or substitute
30 ml/2 tbsp dry sherry
salt and freshly ground white pepper
    to taste

To garnish
1 tbsp slivers sweet red pepper
pinch of paprika

◆ In a large saucepan, melt the butter. Add the celery, onion, thyme, chilli flakes and lemon rind. Cook until the vegetables are softened, stirring once more, about 20 minutes.

◆ Stir in the flour a little at a time. Gradually stir in the stock and milk. Cover and simmer until bubbling and thick, stirring occasionally, about 5–10 minutes.

◆ Add the lobster or fish, cover and cook until opaque, about 5 minutes. Season with sherry, salt and pepper. Garnish with red pepper and paprika.

CATALAN MUSSEL SOUP

The best of Spain's regional mussel soups, this has a hint of
anis, though a big glass of dry white wine can replace the spirits.
The initial part of the recipe also makes a good fish sauce or a
tortilla *filling.*

SERVES 4

1 kg/2 lb mussels
30 ml/2 tbsp olive oil
1 mild Spanish onion, chopped
1 garlic clove, finely chopped
2 big, ripe tomatoes, skinned,
    seeded and chopped
125 ml/4 fl oz anis, *aguardiente* or
    Pernod

salt and freshly ground black pepper
pinch of cayenne pepper
juice of ½ lemon
2 tbsp chopped fresh parsley
4 slices of stale bread

◆ Clean the mussels. Cover them with cold water then scrub them one by one. Pull off all the "beards". Throw out any that are smashed or do not shut when touched.

◆ Meanwhile, heat the oil in a casserole big enough to contain all the ingredients and fry the onion gently, adding the garlic when it softens. Add the chopped tomato flesh and juice to the pan and cook until reduced to a sauce. Add 150 ml/¼ pt of water to the pan.

◆ Add the mussels in 2–3 batches. Cook with the lid on for 3–4 minutes until they open. Then use a slotted spoon to remove them to a plate and discard the top shell of each one. Throw away any that smell really strong or that remain obstinately shut. When they are all done, return them to the pan and sprinkle with the anis, *aguardiente* or Pernod.

◆ Add more water – about 340 ml/⅔ pt – and bring back to simmering. Season with salt and pepper, adding cayenne pepper and lemon juice to taste and parsley. Break a slice of bread into the bottom of each bowl and ladle in the soup.

PRAWN AND LEEK BISQUE

This rich, creamy bisque starts with a flavourful prawn stock, so buy prawns with the heads on if you can find them. It's important to make your own stock for this soup, so it picks up the delicate flavour of leeks. If you can't find prawns with heads, get some extra shells to make the stock with. You can make the soup up to the point of puréeing early in the day, then reheat and add the cream just before serving.

SERVES 6

350 g/12 oz medium prawns, shelled
   and deveined with heads and
   shells reserved
1 large carrot, unpeeled, cubed
2 sticks celery, leaves and all, sliced
2 leeks, including green tops, sliced
2–3 sprigs of fresh parsley
2 bay leaves
5 black peppercorns
40 g/1½ oz butter
1 leek, white part only, chopped
2 cloves garlic, finely chopped
450 g/1 lb mushrooms, sliced

2 tbsp minced fresh parsley
1 bay leaf
1 tsp salt
2 tsp chopped fresh basil
1 tsp chopped fresh thyme
large pinch of white pepper
large pinch of black pepper
large pinch of cayenne pepper
½ tsp dry mustard
20 g/¾ oz plain flour
350 ml/12 fl oz double cream
30 ml/2 tbsp sherry

◆ Put the prawn heads and shells, carrot, celery, leeks, parsley, bay leaves and peppercorns in a large pot. Add 900 ml/1½ pt water. Make a mental note of the water level in the pot, because you will need at least 900 ml/1½ pt of stock after it has simmered for several hours. Add another 900 ml–1.75 litres/1½–3 pt water, enough to cover the prawn shells and vegetables by several inches. Bring to the boil. Skim off the grey foam. Reduce the heat and simmer, uncovered, for 2–3 hours, adding extra water if necessary to keep at least 900 ml/1½ pt liquid in the pot.

◆ Strain the stock, discarding the prawn heads, shells and vegetables. Measure 900 ml/1½ pt stock into a small saucepan; freeze or refrigerate any remaining stock for future use. Return 900 ml/1½ pt stock to the stove and keep warm over a low heat.

◆ In a frying pan, melt the butter. Sauté the leek, garlic and mushrooms about 10 minutes. Add the vegetables to the stock with the seasonings. Bring to the boil, then reduce the heat and simmer, uncovered, 15 minutes. Add the prawns and simmer just until they are opaque and tightly curled.

◆ Purée the soup in a blender or food processor; you will probably have to do this in several batches. (At this point you may refrigerate the puréed soup for several hours. Reheat before continuing.)

◆ Whisk the flour into the cream, then add to the soup. Heat just short of the boiling point. Taste and adjust the seasonings. Add the sherry and serve.

CRABMEAT SOUP

SERVES 5–6

175–200 g/6–7 oz crabmeat, fresh or
    frozen
2 slices fresh root ginger
2 spring onions
1 cake fresh bean curd
225 g/8 oz young spinach
30 ml/2 tbsp vegetable oil

900 ml/1½ pt good stock (see p.12)
1 chicken stock cube
1 tsp salt
pepper to taste
2 tbsp cornflour blended with 5 tbsp
    water

◆ Flake the crabmeat, thawing first if necessary. Coarsely chop the ginger. Cut the spring onions into 1 cm/½ inch shreds. Cut the bean curd into cubes. Wash the spinach, removing any tough stems and discoloured leaves.

◆ Heat the oil in a wok or saucepan. When hot, stir-fry the ginger and spring onion for 30 seconds. Add the crabmeat and stir-fry for 15 seconds. Pour in the stock. Add the crumbled stock cube and the salt and pepper. Bring to the boil, stirring. Add the spinach and bean curd. Bring the contents to the boil again, stirring, then simmer gently for 2 minutes. Stir in the blended cornflour and cook until the soup has thickened.

Starters, Snacks AND Salads

Light bites can range from piquant spring rolls to pickled fish; salads may be composed of tropical fruit, rice or pasta. Each nation has a delightfully different idea of just what constitutes starters, snacks and salads.

ITALIAN

PRAWN SALAD WITH A LITTLE GREEN BATH

SERVES 4

2 very large uncooked prawns
juice of 1 lemon
300 ml/½ pt olive oil
2 tbsp fresh parsley

25 g/1 oz pine kernels
4 large cloves garlic
6 anchovy fillets
4 capers

◆ Peel the prawns and remove the dark, thread-like intestine if you can find it. (This is not essential.) Either discard the shells or set them aside to make soup or stock with later.

◆ Bring a copious quantity of water to the boil – at least 4 times the volume of the prawns. Add the lemon juice and poach the prawns for 3–5 minutes.

◆ Remove the prawns from the liquid and slice each of them in half lengthwise.

◆ There are two ways of making the little green bath. Either put the oil, parsley, pine kernels, garlic, anchovies and capers in a liquidizer and blend until smooth, or very finely chop the parsley, garlic, anchovies and capers; crush the pine kernels, and briskly stir everything into the oil. (In the case of the latter method, leave the mixture to stand for 10 minutes or so in order to enable the flavours to mingle well.)

◆ Serve the prawns with the sauce as a dip.

CARIBBEAN

ISLAND FRUIT SALAD

Add prawns to the marinade and this becomes a regal salad.

SERVES 4

15 ml/1 tbsp balsamic vinegar
juice of 1 orange
10 ml/2 tsp soy sauce
30 ml/2 tbsp vegetable oil
¼ tsp salt
½ tsp sugar (optional)
2 medium oranges, peeled and
    separated into segments,
    reserving juice

150 g/5 oz canned unsweetened
    grapefruit segments, drained
1 starfruit, kiwi or pear, sliced
450 g/1 lb cooked prawns, shelled
    and deveined
1 medium red onion, thinly sliced
lettuce leaves or two avocados, to
    garnish (optional)

◆ In a blender or food processor or by hand, blend the vinegar, orange juice, soy sauce, oil, salt and sugar until smooth. Transfer to a bowl and add the orange and grapefruit segments, starfruit, kiwi or pear slices, prawns and onion. Marinate, covered, in the refrigerator for 1 hour. Drain the fruit and onion of liquid and serve on lettuce-lined plates or in halved, stoned avocados, partially scooped out.

VEGETARIAN CRYSTAL VIETNAMESE ROLLS

The secret is not to wet the Banh Trang too much in case it tears. It will take a bit of practice but it is well worth the effort as guests will be impressed by your efforts.

SERVES 4

225 g/8 oz rice vermicelli
4 dried Chinese mushrooms or
   8 button mushrooms
2 pieces black wood ear fungus
1 packet round Banh Trang rice
   paper
2 pickled onions, thinly sliced
2 pickled gherkins, thinly sliced
225 g/8 oz sliced bamboo shoots,
   drained and thinly sliced
1 carrot, grated
4 rings fresh pineapple or small can
   pineapple slices, drained and
   thinly sliced

Dipping Sauce
100 ml/4 fl oz Nuoc Mam sauce or
   Maggi liquid seasoning; if using
   Maggi add 2 tbsp lemon juice
1 clove garlic, crushed
1 small chilli, chopped (optional)

To serve
1 Webbs or round lettuce
sprigs of coriander
sprigs of mint
½ cucumber, peeled and sliced into
   matchsticks 3 cm/1¼ in long

◆ Make the dipping sauce by combining all the ingredients and mixing thoroughly. Soak the rice vermicelli in boiled water, slightly cooled, until soft. Drain thoroughly.

◆ Soak the dried mushrooms and wood ear fungus in boiled water, slightly cooled, until soft. Drain and squeeze out excess water. If using button mushrooms, wash and dry thoroughly. Slice thinly.

◆ Place a clean tea towel on the surface you are working on. Dip a single sheet of Banh Trang into warm water and place it on the tea towel. It should be soft and pliable but not too wet. Place some vermicelli, dried mushrooms, wood ear fungus, pickled onion, pickled gherkin, bamboo shoots, carrot and pineapple near the centre but towards the bottom edge.

◆ Spread the filling into a sausage shape. Roll the bottom edge of the Banh Trang up and tuck tightly under the mixture. Fold the left and right sides into the centre and continue rolling away from you. Continue until all the mixture is used.

◆ Place the vegetarian rolls on a dish. The guests help themselves to lettuce leaves, one at a time. On the lettuce they place a roll, some mint, coriander and cucumber. They then roll everything and dip it in the dipping sauce.

MANGO-STARFRUIT SALAD WITH GINGER VINAIGRETTE

This vinaigrette tastes great sprinkled over boniato chips, fried green plantains, green salads and even jerk dishes.

SERVES 4

4 mangoes, cubed
4 starfruits, sliced crosswise for star
   shapes
15 g/½ oz root ginger, grated
100 ml/4 fl oz olive oil
100 ml/4 fl oz cider vinegar

30 ml/2 tbsp fresh lime juice
1 tsp French mustard
1 tsp minced fresh coriander
¼ tsp minced spring onion
¼ tsp salt
¼ tsp freshly ground black pepper

◆ Combine the mangoes and starfruit and chill. Purée the ginger, olive oil, vinegar, lime juice, mustard, coriander, spring onion, salt and pepper until smooth in a food processor or blender or by hand. Drizzle over the chilled fruit.

PRAWN-CHORIZO FAJITAS IN LETTUCE

SERVES 4

225 g/8 oz chorizo, casing removed and finely diced

½ sweet green pepper, seeded and diced

½ red pepper, seeded and diced

7 ml/1½ tsp olive oil

225 g/8 oz medium raw prawns, shelled, deveined and diced

20 radicchio leaves

20 stuffed green olives for garnish (optional)

◆ In a large frying pan over medium heat, sauté the chorizo and peppers in oil until the peppers are tender, 8 minutes. Stir in the prawns and sauté for 2 more minutes or until the prawns are no longer translucent.

◆ Spoon about 2 tbsp prawn-chorizo mixture into each radicchio leaf, then roll the leaf and fasten with an olive-studded cocktail toothpick. Serve at once.

PERUVIAN PICKLED FISH

This very contemporary fish dish, also known as ceviche, is popular with Jews in Central and South America. Any firm white fish can be used, as well as salmon, sea trout and even thinly sliced scallops. The acid in the lime and lemon juice has a similar effect to heat; the fish is effectively cooked.

SERVES 4–6

1 kg/2 lb sole, halibut or red snapper fillets, or any combination of firm-fleshed, non-oily fish
250 ml/8 fl oz fresh lemon juice
250 ml/8 fl oz fresh lime juice
2 red chillies, thinly sliced
2 red onions, thinly sliced
1–2 garlic cloves, peeled and finely chopped
kosher salt and freshly ground black pepper to taste
fresh coriander leaves, to garnish

◆ Cut the fish fillets into 2.5 cm/1 in strips and place in a large, shallow, non-metallic dish.

◆ In a large bowl, combine the remaining ingredients except the garnish. Pour the marinade over the fish strips, spreading evenly over the fish. Refrigerate for at least 3 hours, or until the fish strips turn white and opaque. (Do not marinate much longer or the fish will begin to fall apart as the acids continue to break down the proteins in the flesh.)

◆ Serve a few fish strips with some chilli and onion slices on individual plates and garnish with coriander leaves.

HERRING AND APPLE SALAD

Salted herrings and rollmops are widely used in southern Poland where fresh fish rarely makes an appearance in shops or on menus. This salad may be served as an appetizer or as a light main dish. In this recipe the herrings are cut into small strips but traditionally they would be served in large pieces, laid on the other salad ingredients.

SERVES 4

3 salted herring fillets
¼ cucumber, peeled and thinly sliced (about 125 g/4 oz)
½ onion, thinly sliced
1 pickled cucumber, thinly sliced
2 crisp, green eating apples, cored, quartered and thinly sliced
5 ml/1 tsp cider vinegar
1 tbsp chopped fresh dill
60 ml/4 tbsp sour cream

◆ Remove any bones from the herring fillets, then cut them into small strips. Mix the herring, cucumber, onion, pickled cucumber and apple with the vinegar.

◆ Spoon the mixture on to a plate and sprinkle with dill. Trickle the sour cream over the salad and serve at once.

Above: Herring and Apple Salad

MUSHROOM CAVIAR

Eastern Europeans, particularly Russians and Poles, are mushroom fanatics. Dawn expeditions into the wooded countryside in search of fungi are a common sight in autumn.

SERVES 8–10

350 g/12 oz fresh mushrooms (the more varieties, the better – field, shiitake, oyster, girolle, etc), finely chopped

1 medium onion, finely chopped

100 g/4 oz butter

15 ml/1 tbsp dry sherry

75 g/3 oz curd cheese

75 g/3 oz full-fat cream cheese

50 g/2 oz fresh parsley, finely chopped

25 g/1 oz fresh tarragon, finely chopped

25 g/1 oz fresh marjoram, finely chopped

◆ In a large frying pan, sauté the mushrooms and onion in the butter over medium heat, stirring often. When the mushrooms are browned and softened, add the sherry. Remove from the heat.

◆ In a bowl, beat together the two cheeses and herbs. Stir in the mushrooms, onion and their juices. Beat the mixture with a wooden spoon until it is well combined. Spoon the pâté into a small crock, smooth, swirl the top and cover. Chill overnight or up to three days before serving with small rye rounds.

WATERCRESS SALAD WITH ZINGY PEPPER DRESSING

This is not for those who like tame, bland salads. This one has the bitiness of watercress, the sweetness of fresh tomato and a delectable mustardy hot pepper heat. It will enliven any plain main dish.

SERVES 4

2 bunches watercress, washed, trimmed and dried

1 large ripe tomato, cut into bite-sized pieces

1 small onion, thinly sliced, rings separated

15 ml/1 tbsp red wine vinegar

15 ml/1 tbsp chicken stock

15 ml/1 tbsp hot pepper sauce

½ tsp minced garlic

¼ tsp French mustard

salt and freshly ground black pepper

◆ In a large bowl, combine the watercress, tomato and onion. In a small bowl, whisk together the vinegar, chicken stock, hot pepper sauce, garlic and mustard. Season with salt and pepper. Drizzle over the salad and toss gently to coat.

ASPARAGUS WITH PARMESAN AND FRIED EGGS

SERVES 4

1 kg/2 lb fresh asparagus
salt to taste
75 g/3 oz butter
50 g/2 oz freshly-grated Parmesan
   cheese

30 ml/2 tbsp olive oil
4 eggs

◆ Preheat the oven to 190°C/375°F/Gas Mark 5. Trim the coarse whitish ends from the asparagus spears.

◆ Boil the asparagus in salted water for about 10 minutes. (If you can keep the heads above the surface of the water, so much the better. Steamed, they have a better chance of remaining intact.)

◆ Grease the bottom of a flat, oven-proof dish with one-third of the butter. It should be large enough to accommodate the asparagus in two layers only.

◆ When the asparagus has cooked, arrange it in the dish.

◆ Sprinkle the Parmesan over the asparagus and dot it with the remaining butter then bake until the cheese and butter form a light brown crust – about 10 minutes.

◆ In the meantime, heat the olive oil in a pan and fry the eggs carefully. You must not break the yolks.

◆ To serve, divide the asparagus into four portions on heated plates. Slide a fried egg over each portion. The crusty, cheesy asparagus is dipped in the egg yolks and eaten by hand.

VIETNAMESE

VIETNAMESE SPRING ROLLS

These delicious spring rolls should not be confused with the Chinese pancake rolls. Traditionally, Vietnamese people would serve these at a party or a special occasion. They do take a bit of time to make, but the result is well worth the effort.

SERVES 6

100 g/4 oz bean thread
   vermicelli
2 dried Chinese mushrooms or
   4 button mushrooms
2 pieces black wood ear fungus
1 tbsp dried prawns or shrimps or
   8 fresh prawns, finely minced
2 cloves garlic, minced
1 carrot, grated
1 onion, grated
100 g/4 oz pork, minced
15 ml/1 tbsp Nuoc Mam sauce or
   15 ml/1 tbsp light soya sauce with
   2 anchovies crushed into it and a
   dash of lime or lemon juice
black pepper
1 egg, beaten
1 packet of quadrant-shaped or
   round Banh Trang rice paper
vegetable oil for frying

Dipping Sauce
30 ml/2 tbsp Nuoc Mam sauce or
   30 ml/2 tbsp Maggi liquid
   seasoning
1 clove garlic, finely chopped
1 red chilli pepper, finely chopped
10 ml/2 tsp lime or lemon juice
5 ml/1 tsp cider vinegar or wine
   vinegar
1 tsp sugar

To serve
1 Webbs or round lettuce
sprigs of coriander
sprigs of mint

◆ Make the dipping sauce first. Combine all the ingredients in a dish and stir thoroughly.

◆ Soak the vermicelli in boiled water slightly cooled until soft and drain thoroughly. Cut with kitchen scissors to make shorter strands.

◆ Soak the Chinese mushrooms and black wood ear fungus in boiled water that has cooled slightly. When soft, drain thoroughly, gently squeezing out any excess water. Cut finely. If using button mushrooms, wash, drain and chop finely.

◆ Soak the dried prawns or shrimp in boiled water that has cooled slightly until soft and then drain thoroughly. Mince finely. If using fresh prawns, wash, drain and mince.

◆ Place the vermicelli, garlic, carrot, onion, black wood ear fungus, mushrooms, dried prawns or shrimps, minced pork, Nuoc Mam sauce, black pepper and egg in a large mixing bowl. With your hands, mix all the ingredients thoroughly until the mixture is stiff enough to be shaped.

◆ Place some boiled water that has cooled slightly in a large bowl. Spread a clean tea towel on the surface you are going to roll on. If using the quadrant Banh Trang rice paper, take one piece and dip it into the water. Place it on the tea towel. Take another piece of rice paper and repeat. The rice paper should turn soft and pliable. (It is very important not to leave the rice paper too long in the water.)

◆ Place the second piece of rice paper on the first. The rounded edge of the quadrant should be at the bottom facing you and the second piece placed about 5 cm/2 in above but overlapping. Place a small amount of the mixture where the pieces overlap at the bottom. Form the mixture into a sausage shape.

◆ Carefully roll the bottom rounded edge over the mixture, tucking the edge under the mixture. Fold over the left and right sides to the middle, then roll the parcel away from you. Repeat these three steps until all the mixture has been used. Be careful not to pack your rolls with too much mixture and try to roll them as tightly as possible, otherwise they will burst when fried.

◆ If using the round rice paper, pass it through the water and place it on the tea towel. Put some mixture roughly in the centre but closer to the edge nearest to you. Form the mixture into a sausage shape. Fold the bottom edge up and over the mixture, tucking it under the mixture securely. Fold the left and right sides over and then continue rolling away from you. If one piece of round rice paper tears then use two, one on top of the other.

◆ When all the rolls are ready, heat the oil until hot in a large frying pan. Shallow fry, turning frequently, until the mixture is cooked, taking care not to burn the rice paper. If you wish to deep-fry, put less filling in the rolls to ensure it is thoroughly cooked before the outside burns. Drain on kitchen paper.

◆ Place the rolls in the centre of a lettuce leaf, with some mint and coriander. Roll up and dip into the dipping sauce while still hot.

TAGLIATELLE NESTS

These make a good first course or a light lunch.

SERVES 4

350 g/12 oz fresh tagliatelle verdi
2 tomatoes, peeled, seeded and
    diced
30 ml/2 tbsp walnut oil
45 ml/3 tbsp sunflower oil
juice of 1 lime
salt and freshly ground black pepper

1 tbsp chopped mint
225 g/8 oz rindless streaky bacon
100 g/4 oz shelled fresh peas
4 small courgettes
4 tbsp sour cream or fromage frais
mint sprigs, to garnish (optional)

◆ Cook the tagliatelle in boiling salted water for 3 minutes, then drain well and turn into a bowl. Add the tomatoes, both types of oil, the lime juice, some seasoning and the mint. Toss well, cover and leave to cool.

◆ Grill the bacon rashers until they are crisp, turning once. Drain them on absorbent kitchen paper and leave to cool. Cook the peas in boiling water for 15 minutes, then drain and set aside. Trim the courgettes, peel them very thinly so that they are a bright green outside, then halve them lengthwise. Slice the courgettes thinly and mix them with the peas.

◆ Divide the tagliatelle and its dressing between four plates, swirling it into nests. Top the nests with the courgette and pea mixture. Crush the crisply grilled bacon and sprinkle it over the courgette and pea mixture, then top with a little sour cream or fromage frais. Mint sprigs may be added as a garnish, if liked.

ITALIAN

SPAGHETTI AND SALAMI SALAD

SERVES 4

350 g/12 oz fresh spaghetti
4 tbsp pine kernels
175 g/6 oz salami, cut in strips
50 g/2 oz black olives, pitted and
    sliced
425 g/15 oz can artichoke hearts,
    drained

30 ml/2 tbsp cider vinegar
salt and freshly ground black pepper
½ tsp caster sugar
90 ml/6 tbsp olive oil
4 tbsp chopped parsley

◆ Cut the spaghetti into 5 cm/2 in lengths, then cook it in boiling salted water for 3 minutes. Drain the pasta well in a fine sieve before tipping it into a bowl; leave to cool.

◆ Roast the pine kernels in a small, dry, heavy-based saucepan until they are lightly browned, then tip them over the pasta. Add the salami, olives and artichoke hearts. Mix the cider vinegar, seasoning and caster sugar in a screw-top jar. Shake well until the sugar dissolves, then add the olive oil and shake again.

◆ Pour the dressing over the salad and mix well. Toss the parsley in after the dressing, immediately before serving the salad.

CHOPPED LIVER

This is probably the most well-known and best-loved Jewish dish. No one really knows its origins, but when it comes to chopped liver, everybody's an expert. Traditionally, chicken fat is used to cook the onions and bind the mixture, as well as provide a smooth texture. This version replaces the fat with vegetable oil which is less rich and lower in saturated fat. Use a kosher margarine if you prefer. Serve with rye bread, challah or matzo. For an elegant presentation, pipe on to small toasts or crackers.

SERVES 6–8

450 g/1 lb chicken livers
salt and freshly ground black pepper
30 ml/2 tbsp vegetable oil
2 medium onions, chopped
4 large eggs, hard-boiled and
    chopped
chicken stock (optional)

To garnish
shredded lettuce
cherry tomatoes

◆ Preheat the grill. Arrange the livers on a foil-lined grill pan and sprinkle with salt. Grill until lightly brown, 3–4 minutes. Turn the livers over, sprinkle with salt and grill until just cooked through, 3–4 minutes longer; the livers should no longer be pink. Remove the livers to a cooling rack to drain and cool slightly.

◆ In a large frying pan, over medium heat, heat the oil. Add the chopped onions and cook until soft and golden, 10–12 minutes, stirring occasionally.

◆ In a food processor fitted with a metal blade, chop the livers coarsely, using the pulse action. Add the onions and, using the pulse action, chop until the livers and onions are just blended. Add the chopped eggs and salt and pepper to taste and, using the pulse action, chop again until just blended. If the mixture is dry, add a little more oil or a spoonful of chicken stock.

◆ Spoon the mixture into a serving bowl, cover and refrigerate for 2 hours or until ready to serve. Garnish with shredded lettuce and cherry tomatoes.

JEWISH

CHEESE KNISHES

Knishes, tiny filled pastries, are multipurpose, traditional Ashkenazic fare. Sometimes served with soup or on their own as an appetizer, they are traditionally eaten at Shavuot with a moist cheese filling. Other fillings include potato, chicken and kasha (buckwheat). Many different kinds of pastry can be used but this sour cream pastry made in the food processor makes the whole job quick and easy.

MAKES ABOUT 2 DOZEN

Pastry
250 g/8 oz plain flour
1 tsp baking powder
½ tsp salt
1 tsp icing sugar
125 g/4 oz unsalted butter or hard
    margarine, cut into small pieces
75 ml/2½ fl oz sour cream
1 egg, beaten, to glaze

Cheese Filling
250 g/8 oz tub cottage cheese
2 tbsp sour cream
2 tbsp fine matzo meal
1 tbsp sugar
1 tbsp melted butter
2 eggs, beaten
45 g/1½ oz sultanas, or 1 tbsp
    chopped fresh parsley

◆ Sift the flour, baking powder, salt and sugar into a large bowl. Transfer to a food processor fitted with a metal blade. Add the butter and process until the mixture resembles fine crumbs. Remove the cover and spoon the sour cream evenly over the flour-butter mixture. Using pulse action, process until the mixture begins to hold together. Do not allow the dough to form into a ball or the pastry will be tough. If the dough appears too dry, add a little cold water, 15 ml/1 tbsp at a time.

◆ Turn out the dough on to a lightly floured work surface and knead lightly. Form into a ball and flatten; wrap well and refrigerate for 2 hours or overnight. Leave the dough to soften for 15 minutes at room temperature before rolling out.

◆ Combine all the filling ingredients until well blended.

◆ Grease two large baking sheets. Cut the dough in half and work with one half at a time. Roll out the dough to a 20 × 30 cm/8 × 12 in rectangle about 3mm/⅛ in thick. Cut into 10 cm/4 in squares. Place filling in the centre of each square.

◆ Brush the edges of each square with a little egg glaze and fold the lower-left corner up to the upper-right corner to form a triangle. Using a fork, press the edges together to seal well. Place on a baking sheet. Continue with the remaining dough and filling. You will need to bake in batches.

◆ Preheat the oven to 200°C/400°F/Gas Mark 6. Brush each triangle with a little egg glaze and score the top of the pastry to let steam escape. Bake until a rich golden brown, 17–20 minutes. Cool for 15 minutes before serving.

NOTE: Smaller knishes can be made by using a 7.5 cm/3 in round cutter and cutting circles from pastry. Fold over 1 spoonful of filling to make a half-moon shape and proceed as above.

SPICY BLACK BEAN AND HAM HOCK SALAD

This tastes best made from scratch, but if you're in a hurry, here's a no-cook version: simply substitute 2 × 450 g/1 lb cans beans, drained and rinsed, and stir in ground versions of the spices and any minced cooked ham or pork. Whip up the vinaigrette in the same manner as below.

SERVES 4

225 g/8 oz black beans
2 large ham hocks
1 large bay leaf
1 tsp coriander seeds, cracked
1 tsp cumin seeds, crushed
1 tsp red chilli pepper flakes
¼ tsp ground cinnamon
50 ml/2 fl oz lime juice
15 ml/1 tbsp sherry vinegar
1 tsp ground cumin

15 ml/1 tbsp olive oil
15 ml/1 tbsp hot pepper sauce
1 clove garlic, crushed
2 tbsp finely chopped sweet red pepper
2 tbsp finely chopped spring onion
salt and freshly ground black pepper
25 g/1 oz fresh coriander, stems removed, rinsed and dried

◆ Soak the beans, if necessary, according to the directions on the packet. Place the beans in a large heavy-based saucepan. Add the ham hocks, bay leaf, coriander seeds, cumin seeds, chilli flakes and cinnamon. Add fresh cold water to cover. Simmer gently over medium heat until the beans are tender, about 45 minutes. Remove the ham hocks and set aside to cool. Remove the bay leaf and discard. Drain the beans and rinse under cold running water until chilled. Set aside.

◆ Combine the lime juice and sherry vinegar in a non-reactive bowl. Whisk in the ground cumin, olive oil, hot pepper sauce and garlic. Stir in the red pepper, spring onion and salt and pepper to taste. Set aside.

◆ Pull the ham off the hock, discarding the bone and fat. Mince the meat and place it in a salad bowl. Add the beans and coriander. Pour the vinaigrette over the mixture and toss to combine. Season to taste with salt, pepper and additional hot sauce.

ENSALADA DE MOROS Y CRISTIANOS

When Cubans serve black beans and rice together, they call it Moros y Christianos – Moors and Christians – after the Saracens who invaded Christian Spain in the 8th century AD.

SERVES 4–6

575 g/1¼ lb cooked or canned black beans, rinsed and drained
350 g/12 oz cooked white long-grain rice
50 g/2 oz chopped fresh coriander
60 ml/4 tbsp freshly squeezed lime juice

175 ml/6 fl oz olive oil
1 small onion, chopped
2 cloves garlic, chopped
salt and freshly ground black pepper to taste

◆ In a bowl, mix together the beans, rice and coriander. Place the lime juice in a small bowl and whisk in the oil. Add the onion and garlic and then toss with the beans. Add salt and pepper to taste.

PAPAYA-CITRUS SALAD WITH PAPAYA SEED DRESSING

This cool and refreshing salad is a nice foil for a spicy jerked dish. The dressing is quite versatile – make an extra batch and use on coleslaw, fruit or green salad.

SERVES 4

1 small red onion, halved and thinly sliced

1 orange, separated into segments, with 30 ml/2 tbsp juice reserved

2 grapefruits, preferably pink, separated into segments

½ ripe papaya (about 225 g/8 oz), coarsely sliced

1 sweet red pepper, cored, seeded and thinly sliced

1 sweet yellow pepper, cored, seeded and thinly sliced

Dressing

60 g/2½ oz sugar

1½ tsp salt

¼ tsp French mustard

45 ml/3 tbsp white vinegar

100 ml/4 fl oz vegetable oil

2 tbsp papaya seeds

◆ Place the onion in a small bowl. Cover with ice water and leave to stand for 30 minutes at room temperature. Drain and dry on absorbent kitchen paper.

◆ Combine the orange and grapefruit segments with the onion, papaya, red pepper and yellow pepper in a large salad bowl.

◆ In a blender or food processor, blend together the sugar, salt, mustard and vinegar until blended well. With the motor running, add the oil in a stream and blend until smooth. Add the seeds and blend until they are about the size of peppercorns. Drizzle the dressing over the salad and toss well.

NUEVO CUBANO

FRUITED CRAB SALAD

O cean sticks or crab sticks work well in this salad because when served cold in a no-cook dish, they are very similar to more expensive crabmeat. Of course, if you prefer to use real crabmeat, by all means do so. If using fresh pineapple, cut lengthwise into quarters, cutting through the crown. Remove the fruit from the shells, discard the core and reserve the shells to use as "pineapple boats".

SERVES 4

1 large fresh pineapple, or 450 g/
    16 oz can unsweetened
    pineapple, cut into bite-sized
    chunks, drained
1 kg/2 lb crabmeat, cut into chunks,
    or ocean sticks or crab sticks

1 large mango, peeled and cubed
225 g/8 oz orange-flesh melon balls
225 g/8 oz seedless grapes
yoghurt or sour cream to serve
    (optional)

◆ Combine the pineapple, crabmeat, mango, orange-flesh melon balls and grapes. Place in your pineapple boats or in a glass bowl. Chill until ready to serve. Serve with yoghurt or, alternatively, with sour cream, if desired.

Meat

Hearty dishes from Spain, hot ones from the Caribbean and India, stir-fried ones from the Far East — there are many ways of presenting a meat dish.

SPANISH

FRIED LAMB WITH PAPRIKA AND VINEGAR

SERVES 4

1 slice stale bread
45 ml/3 tbsp red wine vinegar
30–60 ml/2–4 tbsp olive oil
800 g/1¾ lb tender lean lamb
   shoulder, diced
salt and freshly ground black pepper
6 garlic cloves

1 *guindilla,* or ½ dried chilli, seeded
   and chopped, or a pinch of
   cayenne pepper
6 cloves
4 tbsp chopped fresh parsley
1 tbsp paprika

◆ Sprinkle the bread with vinegar. Fry it in a casserole in 30 ml/ 2 tbsp hot oil and reserve. Season the lamb with black pepper and salt. Put the casserole over your hottest burner and add the meat in handfuls, with 3 finely chopped garlic cloves and the *guindilla,* chilli, or cayenne pepper, turning it and keeping it moving with a wooden spoon. Add more lamb as each batch is sealed, with more oil as necessary.

◆ Crush 3 garlic cloves in a mortar (or an electric herb or coffee mill). Then crush in the cloves and fresh parsley, reducing everything to a paste.

◆ Sprinkle the lamb with paprika, stirring in the paste and 200 ml/ 7 fl oz of water. Cook, covered, until the lamb is tender (about 30 minutes) and the liquid reduced to a few spoonfuls. Finally purée the reserved bread and stir in to thicken the sauce. Check the seasonings before serving.

VIETNAMESE

LAMB'S LIVER WITH GINGER AND CORIANDER

SERVES 4

450 g/1 lb lamb's liver, cut into
   4 cm/1½ in wide strips and cut
   again crosswise into strips
   5 mm/⅛ in thick
30 ml/2 tbsp vegetable oil
1 large onion, cut into wedges about
   4 cm/1½ in wide
2 medium sweet green peppers,
   halved
salt
15 ml/1 tbsp sesame oil

30 ml/2 tbsp rice wine or dry sherry
2 tsp sugar
2 large cloves garlic, coarsely
   chopped
1 tbsp fermented black beans, rinsed
   and coarsely chopped
2 x 2.5 cm/1 in slices root ginger,
   peeled and minced
1 tbsp fresh coriander, chopped
1 spring onion, coarsely chopped
2 tsp cornflour mixed with
   30 ml/2 tbsp water

Sauce
30 ml/2 tbsp Nuoc Mam sauce or
   light soy sauce

◆ Bring a large saucepan half full of water to the boil. Put in the liver slices and stir until the water begins to puff into a boil again. Drain the liver and hold under the cold water tap to stop the cooking. Drain and set aside.

◆ Combine the Nuoc Mam sauce, rice wine and sugar and stir until the sugar dissolves.

◆ Heat a wok over high heat and add 15 ml/1 tbsp oil. Scatter in the onions and peppers and stir and toss vigorously until they are shining. Sprinkle in some salt and stir for about 1 minute until the onions are translucent. Transfer to a dish.

◆ Wipe the wok, add the remaining oil and put in the garlic, black beans, ginger, coriander and spring onions and stir for about 30 seconds to sear them. Add the liver slices to the wok and stir for a further 30 seconds.

◆ Add the Nuoc Mam mixture and toss and turn the meat. Add the cooked vegetables and stir them around so they integrate with the meat. Add the cornflour to the wok, a little at a time, stirring constantly. Sprinkle in the sesame oil, toss a couple of times, and ladle out on a hot serving dish.

TUNG-PO MUTTON

SERVES 4–6

225 g/8 oz stewing mutton or lamb
125 g/4 oz potato
125 g/4 oz carrot
oil for deep-frying
30 ml/2 tbsp soya sauce
15 g/½ oz sugar

2 spring onions
1 slice fresh root ginger
1 clove garlic, crushed
½ tsp Sichuan pepper
1 tsp five-spice powder
45 ml/3 tbsp rice wine or dry sherry

◆ Cut the mutton into 2 cm/¾ in cubes, then score one side of each square halfway down. Peel the potato and carrot and cut them the same size and shape as the mutton.

◆ Heat up quite a lot of oil in a wok or deep-fryer. When it is smoking, deep-fry the mutton for 5–6 seconds or until it turns golden; scoop out and drain, then fry the potato and carrot, also until golden.

◆ Place the mutton in a pot or casserole, cover the meat with cold water, add the soya sauce, sugar, spring onions, root ginger, garlic, pepper, five-spice powder and rice wine or sherry, and bring it to a boil. Then reduce the heat and simmer for 2–3 hours; add the potato and carrot, cook together for about 5 minutes and serve.

ITALIAN

ROAST RABBIT WITH LAMB

This recipe links two meats with very different, but highly complementary, basic qualities.

SERVES 8–10

1 large lamb shoulder (weighing about 2 kg/4½ lb), cut into 8 large bone-in chunks
1 large rabbit, jointed into 8–4 legs with the saddle cut into 4 pieces
1 large onion, sliced

4 cloves garlic, roughly crushed
4 good sprigs rosemary
12 fresh sage leaves
300 ml/½ pt dry white wine
60 ml/4 tbsp dry Marsala
salt and freshly ground black pepper

◆ Preheat the oven to 180°C/550°F/Gas Mark 4. Heat a baking tray to very hot. Add no oil. Drop in the lamb shoulder. Seal the lamb pieces by sautéeing very fiercely, then lower the heat until a little of the lamb fat begins to run. Remove the lamb and set aside.
◆ Add the jointed rabbit. Seal the rabbit gently for 2–3 minutes. Remove and set aside.
◆ Scorch the onion in what should be a very lightly-greased baking tray. Add the garlic, rosemary, sage and the wines. Bring everything to the boil.
◆ Replace the meat, making sure the pieces alternate with each other: the fat of the lamb must moisten the rabbit during the cooking process and the flavour of the rabbit must permeate the lamb. Season at this point.
◆ Cover and bake in the oven for about 1½ hours.

SPANISH

FRIED LAMB WITH LEMON JUICE

The lamb of Old Castile is a wonder. In restaurants the animal is baked whole in great domed ovens. At home it is more likely to be fried simply with lemon juice. This is one of the nicest ways to cook fatless meat.

SERVES 4

850 g/1¾ lb trimmed tender lamb, in strips
salt and freshly ground black pepper
30 ml/2 tbsp olive oil
1 onion, chopped

2 cloves garlic, finely chopped
2 tsp paprika
250 ml/8 fl oz stock or water
juice of 1 lemon
2 tbsp finely chopped parsley

◆ Season the lamb with salt and pepper. Heat the oil in a casserole over your hottest burner and add the meat in handfuls. Add the onion, too, and keep turning the meat around with a wooden spoon. Add more meat as each batch is sealed, with the garlic and more oil if necessary.
◆ When the meat is golden and the onion is soft, sprinkle with paprika and add the stock or water. Continue cooking over a medium heat until the liquid has virtually gone.
◆ Sprinkle with the lemon juice and parsley, cover and simmer for 5 minutes. Check the seasonings before serving.

CHINESE

LAMB IN SWEET AND SOUR SAUCE

SERVES 4–6

225 g/8 oz lamb fillet
2 slices root ginger, peeled
15 g/½ oz cornflour
1 tbsp yellow bean sauce
22 ml/1½ tbsp soya sauce

15 ml/1 tbsp rice wine or sherry
15 ml/1 tbsp vinegar
25 g/1 oz sugar
oil for deep-frying
½ tsp chicken fat or sesame seed oil

◆ Thinly slice the lamb and finely chop the root ginger.

◆ Mix the lamb with a quarter of the cornflour, a little water and the yellow bean sauce.
◆ Mix the remaining cornflour with the soya sauce, rice wine or sherry, vinegar, sugar and the finely chopped root ginger.
◆ Heat up the oil in a wok or pan, fry the lamb slices for about 15 seconds and stir to separate them. When they turn pale, scoop them out and then return them to the wok over a high heat. Add the sauce mixture, stir and blend well for about 1 minute; add chicken fat or sesame seed oil, stir a few more times, then serve.

Above: Fried Lamb with Lemon Juice

SAUTÉED LAMB WITH AUBERGINE IN A SAUCE

SERVES 4

2 large aubergines, ends cut off,
   thickly sliced
45 ml/3 tbsp olive oil
8 lamb cutlets, trimmed
2 cloves garlic, crushed
6 large tomatoes, blanched, skinned
   and thickly sliced
salt and freshly ground black pepper

Sauce
2 tbsp fresh mint, chopped
150 ml/¼ pt natural yoghurt
freshly ground black pepper

To garnish
1 lemon, sliced
sprigs of mint

◆ Sprinkle salt over the aubergine and leave for 20 minutes. Rinse the aubergine and dry with absorbent kitchen paper.

◆ Heat 30 ml/2 tbsp olive oil in a wok over a very high heat and add the lamb cutlets. When brown, lower the heat and continue cooking until the meat is tender – about 5 minutes on each side. Remove from the wok, drain on absorbent kitchen paper and keep in a warm oven.

◆ Add the remaining oil to the wok and fry the aubergine slices with the garlic until they are lightly browned on both sides. (If the oil dries out, add a little more.) When they are cooked, push them up the side of the wok and add the tomato slices. Stir-fry for a few moments and season with salt and pepper.

◆ Place the vegetables on a dish and arrange the cutlets over the vegetables. Garnish with lemon slices and sprigs of mint.

◆ Prepare the sauce by stirring the mint into the yoghurt. Grind some black pepper over it and serve in a small bowl.

RED-COOKED LAMB

This recipe appears to be rather elaborate but, if followed correctly, it will taste like nothing on earth! If you tasted it blindfolded you would never be able to guess what you were eating, but nevertheless you would marvel at the delicious flavour of this dish.

SERVES 4–6

750 g/1½ lb lamb fillet in one piece
30 ml/½ tbsp soya sauce
oil for deep frying
30 ml/2 tbsp rice wine (or sherry)
1 tsp salt
1½ tbsp Chinese dried dates, soaked

175 g/6 oz water chestnuts, peeled
2 slices root ginger, peeled
2 spring onions, cut into short lengths
½ tsp five-spice powder
1.8 litres/3 pt stock
1 tbsp cornflour
½ tsp sesame seed oil

◆ Wash the lamb fillet thoroughly; make a succession of cuts two-thirds of the way through the piece of meat at 1 cm/½ in intervals. Blanch the meat in boiling water for about 3 minutes, then drain it well and coat it with soya sauce.

◆ Place the meat in a strainer and lower it into oil to deep-fry over a moderate heat for about 1½ minutes or until it turns red; remove and drain.

◆ Pour off the excess oil; put the meat back with rice wine or sherry, salt, dates, water chestnuts, ginger root, onions, soya sauce, five-spice powder and stock; bring to a boil, then transfer to a casserole. Simmer gently for 1½ hours or until the stock is reduced by half; add the mushrooms and cook for another 10 minutes or so. Now remove the meat and cut it into 1 cm/½ in thick pieces. Place the water chestnuts, dates and mushrooms on a serving dish with the lamb pieces on top.

◆ Remove the onions and ginger root from the gravy and discard them; warm up about 250 ml/8 fl oz of the gravy in a small saucepan. Add sesame seed oil and thicken it with a little cornflour; stir to make it smooth, then pour it over the lamb and serve.

BEEF AND VEGETABLE ROLLS

SERVES 4

1 medium carrot	**Sauce**
125 g/4 oz asparagus	1 tbsp sugar
125 g/4 oz French beans	45 ml/3 tbsp water
350 g/12 oz prime beef, sliced	15 ml/1 tbsp sake
paper-thin	15 ml/1 tbsp mirin
cornflour or potato flour	45 ml/3 tbsp soy sauce
vegetable oil	

◆ Scrape the carrot and cut into long, narrow strips. Trim the asparagus. Top and tail the beans.

◆ Parboil the vegetables separately in lightly salted water until just tender. Drain and refresh in cold water. Drain and pat dry.

◆ On a chopping board, lay half the meat slices side by side with edges overlapping to form a sheet of even width. Press the overlapping sections gently so that they stick. Brush with cornflour.

◆ Lay a few strips of each vegetable at one end of the beef sheet. Roll up firmly. Tie securely with white cotton string. Repeat the process with the remaining beef and vegetables.

◆ Combine the sauce ingredients in a bowl and stir well to blend. Put a little oil into a frying pan and heat over high heat. Add the rolls and sauté until lightly browned.

◆ Pour the sauce over the rolls and bring to a simmer. Continue to simmer over low heat for 5 minutes, until the beef is tender.

◆ To serve, cut the strings and slice the rolls into 2.5 cm/1 in rounds. Arrange on 4 dishes and spoon over a little of the sauce.

OLD-FASHIONED POT ROAST WITH ONION GRAVY

SERVES 8–10

2.25–2.7 kg/5–6 lb brisket of beef or	salt and freshly ground black pepper
boneless beef shoulder	½ tsp dried thyme
1 tbsp plain flour	½ tsp paprika
60 ml/4 tbsp vegetable oil	1 bay leaf
6 onions, cut into 1 cm/½ in rings	6 carrots, cut into 6 mm/¼ in slices
4–6 cloves garlic, peeled and finely	on the diagonal
chopped	fresh parsley sprigs, to garnish
250 ml/8 fl oz tomato juice	

◆ Rinse the meat under cold running water; pat dry with absorbent kitchen paper. Trim any visible fat, then dust the meat with flour.

◆ In a large ovenproof casserole, over medium-high heat, heat 30 ml/2 tbsp oil. Add the meat and cook until browned on underside, 5–7 minutes. Turn the meat and cook until the other side is browned, 5–6 minutes longer. Remove to a plate.

◆ Preheat the oven to 170°C/325°F/Gas Mark 3. Add the remaining oil to the casserole and stir in the onions. Cook until the onions begin to soften and colour, 4–5 minutes. Add the garlic and cook for 1 minute longer. Pour in the tomato juice, stirring and scraping to pick up any bits from the bottom. Season with salt and pepper to taste, thyme, paprika and bay leaf.

◆ Return the beef to the casserole and add enough water to cover all the ingredients. Bring to a boil and skim off any foam that comes to the surface. Cover tightly and cook in the oven until the beef is fork-tender, 3–3½ hours. Add the carrots to the pot and cook until tender, 30 minutes longer.

◆ Remove the casserole from the oven and remove the lid. If the liquid is too thin, remove the beef to a deep serving platter and reduce the gravy to thicken slightly. Spoon the gravy with onions and carrots around the beef and garnish with parsley. Serve the meat carved into 6 mm/¼ in slices.

> NOTE: As with all slowly cooked stews and meats, this dish is best cooked a day ahead. Refrigerate and skim off congealed fat. Reheat in a 180°C/350°F/Gas Mark 4 oven for 35–40 minutes.

Above: Old Fashioned Pot Roast with Onion Gravy

BRAISED BEEF WITH BROCCOLI

SERVES 4

200 g/7 oz sirloin of beef, thinly sliced	30 ml/2 tbsp vegetable oil
300 g/11 oz broccoli	30 ml/1 tbsp each sake, rice vinegar,
125 g/4 oz button mushrooms	sesame seed oil, water and sugar
2 cloves garlic	2 tsp cornflour

◆ With a sharp knife, cut the beef into small even chunks. Wash and trim the broccoli and divide into florets. Wipe and trim the mushrooms and halve them. Peel the garlic and slice finely.

◆ Heat the oil in a large saucepan over medium heat. Add the garlic and fry for a few minutes to flavour the oil. Add the mushrooms and sauté lightly. Stir in the broccoli and beef and sauté to brown the beef. Add the remaining ingredients and bring to the boil.

◆ Cover with a drop lid and simmer over medium heat for 5 minutes until the beef is cooked, occasionally ladling the sauce over the beef. Arrange in small, deep serving bowls to serve, and ladle over a little of the stock.

SLICED SIMMERED BEEF WITH TURNIPS AND CARROTS

SERVES 6

salt and freshly ground black pepper

1–2 tbsp paprika

1.5 kg/3 lb beef rump, shoulder or shank, tied in one piece

25 g/1 oz lard

3 onions, chopped

200 g/7 oz *tocino,* unsmoked bacon, salt or fresh pork belly, cubed

1 piece of bone, such as a bit of beef shin or gammon knuckle

4 carrots, thickly sliced

4 small turnips, chopped

2 sprigs of thyme

4 parsley stalks, bruised, plus 2 tbsp chopped parsley

1 sprig of mint

1 bay leaf

150 ml/¼ pt red wine

150 ml/¼ pt red wine vinegar

◆ Rub salt, pepper and the paprika into the beef. Heat the lard in a deep casserole, which should be the right size to take everything neatly, and brown the meat on all sides. Then put the chopped onions round the meat and allow them to soften, adding the pork cubes and stirring occasionally.

◆ Fit the bone, carrots, turnips and the herbs (preferably tied round with a bit of cotton) into the casserole. Then add a little more seasoning and also the chopped parsley. Pour in the wine and vinegar and bring to simmering, uncovered. Fit a piece of foil securely under the lid and simmer very gently for 1½ hours until the meat is cooked.

◆ Move to a serving plate and let the meat rest for 10 minutes before it is eaten.

◆ Carve the meat in slices and arrange the vegetables and pork around them. Discard the bone and herbs. Blend the contents of the casserole and return to the pot to rewarm. Check the seasonings. Pour some gravy over the meat and pass the rest round in a sauce boat. Sprinkle with parsley.

SHREDDED BEEF WITH CELERY

SERVES 4–6

225 g/8 oz beef steak

50 g/2 oz celery

50 g/2 oz leek or spring onion

2 slices fresh root ginger

45 ml/3 tbsp oil

15 ml/1 tbsp chilli paste

30 ml/2 tbsp soya sauce

½ tsp salt

1 tsp sugar

15 ml/1 tbsp rice wine or dry sherry

5 ml/1 tsp vinegar

◆ Shred the beef into thin matchstick-sized strips. Shred the celery and leeks the same size (Chinese leeks are a cross between the Western leek and spring onion with thin skin and green foliage). Peel the root ginger and cut it into thin shreds.

◆ Heat up the wok or pan and put in the oil. When it starts to smoke, stir-fry the beef for a short while, add the chilli paste, blend well, then add the celery, leek and root ginger, followed by the soya sauce, salt, sugar and wine. Stir for 1–2 minutes, add vinegar and serve.

MEAT CURRY WITH NUTS AND COCONUT MILK

SERVES 4

flesh of 1 coconut, grated
50 g/2 oz cashew nuts
2 cloves garlic, chopped
½ tsp chilli powder
15 g/½ oz fresh ginger, grated
½ tsp ground coriander
½ tsp turmeric
leaves from 1 sprig of coriander
½ tsp garam masala

½ tsp ground pepper
125 g/4 oz butter or ghee
1 small onion, chopped
1 kg/2 lb meat, trimmed and cubed
¼ tsp saffron
25 g/1 oz sultanas
50 g/2 oz almonds
salt
4–6 curry leaves

◆ Blend the coconut in a liquidizer with 1 tbsp boiling water. Transfer to a sheet of muslin and squeeze out the milk into a bowl. Return the coconut to the liquidizer and repeat the process.

◆ Grind, pound or blend in a liquidizer the cashew nuts, garlic, chilli powder, ginger, ground coriander, turmeric, coriander leaves, garam masala and pepper.

◆ Heat the butter or ghee in a pan, add the onion and fry until golden, then add the blended spices and fry for a further 5 minutes.

◆ Add the meat, stir and fry for 5 minutes, then pour on the coconut milk, add the saffron, sultanas, almonds and ½ tsp salt and cook, covered, over a low heat for about 1 hour, until the meat is tender and the sauce has thickened.

◆ Sprinkle on the curry leaves.

BEEF IN COCONUT MILK

SERVES 4

30 ml/2 tbsp vegetable oil
1 clove garlic, crushed
225 g/8 oz topside of beef, thinly sliced
1 small onion, thinly sliced
pinch of turmeric
½ green chilli pepper

1 cm/½ in lemon grass, cut from the bottom, thinly sliced
15 ml/1 tbsp canned coconut milk

To garnish
1 tbsp peanuts, crushed
handful of fresh coriander, chopped

◆ Heat the oil until very hot. Add the garlic. When the smell is released, add everything except the coconut milk. Stir-fry for about 3 minutes or until the meat is cooked.

◆ Add the coconut milk and stir once. Serve garnished with crushed peanuts and chopped coriander.

MEAT CURRY WITH ROASTED SPICES

SERVES 4

45 ml/3 tbsp oil
2 tbsp coriander seeds
2 red chillies, cut into pieces
2.5 cm/1 in cinnamon stick
3 cloves
50 g/2 oz grated coconut
450 g/1 lb meat, trimmed and cubed
½ tsp turmeric
salt

2 green chillies, sliced
15 g/½ oz fresh ginger, grated
1 small onion, chopped
225 g/8 oz potatoes, peeled and
  diced
225 g/8 oz tomatoes, peeled and
  chopped
900 ml/1½ pt boiling water
6 curry leaves

◆ Heat half the oil in a pan and fry the coriander seeds, red chilli, cinnamon, cloves and coconut for about 5 minutes, then transfer to a grinder or a mortar and reduce to a smooth paste.

◆ Put the meat in a bowl with the turmeric, ½ tsp salt, green chilli, ginger and half the onion. Add the spice paste and mix well. Leave to marinate for 15 minutes.

◆ Heat the remaining oil in a large saucepan and fry the remaining onion until golden.

◆ Add the marinated meat, the potato and tomato, pour on the boiling water, cover and cook on a low heat for about 1 hour, until the meat is tender and the sauce is thick.

◆ Add extra salt to taste and sprinkle on the curry leaves.

BEEF STROGANOFF

The Stroganovs became one of the wealthiest members of Russia's merchant aristocracy through their exploitation of Siberia's fur resources. The French chef of a late 19th-century Count Stroganov created this now internationally popular dish. It should not be served over rice – a heresy introduced by the West – but a tuft of straw potatoes on top is classically acceptable.

SERVES 6–8

1 tbsp dry mustard powder
1 tbsp sugar
90 ml/6 tbsp sunflower oil
3 large onions, sliced
450 g/1 lb fresh button or field
   mushrooms, sliced
1.25 kg/2½ lb fresh beef fillet, cut
   into 1 cm/½ in wide strips

salt and freshly ground black pepper
600 ml/1 pt sour cream
6 fresh parsley sprigs, stems
   removed, chopped
deep-fried straw potatoes (optional)

◆ Combine the mustard and sugar in a bowl with water to make a paste. Let the flavours mingle while completing the recipe.

◆ Heat half the sunflower oil in a large, heavy-bottomed shallow casserole. When just crackling, add the sliced onions, reduce the heat to low, and stir. Gently soften the onions, covered, for about 25 minutes, stirring occasionally. During the last 10 minutes, uncover and add the mushrooms. Remove from the heat, drain the mixture, and set aside in a bowl.

◆ Heat the remaining oil in the casserole. Drop in half the meat, stirring with a wooden spoon and turning the strips over to brown evenly. Transfer with a slotted spoon to the bowl with the vegetables; sauté the remaining meat. When all is browned, return the meat and vegetables to the casserole, together with the mustard mixture. Season to taste and add the sour cream, a little at a time, stirring continuously. Cover the casserole, heat through gently for about 5 minutes, and serve. Top each serving with a light scattering of parsley, and the straw potatoes, if desired.

SPICY BEEF STEW

This particular stew is, arguably, Vietnam's boeuf à la bourguignonne.

SERVES 4

45 ml/3 tbsp vegetable oil
2 medium onions, finely chopped
5 cloves garlic, finely chopped
10 spring onions, dead skin peeled off
1 stalk lemon grass, cut into 5 cm/2 in sections and crushed
1 kg/2 lb stewing beef, cut into 2.5 cm/1 in cubes

1.2 litres/2 pt water
90 ml/3½ fl oz yellow bean sauce
1 tsp chilli powder
4 star anise
2.5 cm/1 in cinnamon stick
½ tsp whole peppercorns
sugar

◆ Heat 15 ml/1 tbsp oil in a wok over a medium high heat. Put in the onions, garlic and whole spring onions and stir-fry for 2 minutes. Add the lemon grass and continue to stir until the onions become lightly brown, remove the spring onions and set aside.

◆ Heat the remaining oil over a high heat. Stir-fry as many pieces of beef as are convenient until they are brown, turning them over from time to time. Continue until all the beef has been cooked.

◆ Add the water. Add the lemon grass mixture, yellow bean sauce, chilli powder, star anise, cinnamon, peppercorns and sugar and bring to the boil. Cover and lower the heat to simmer for 1½ hours.

◆ Add the spring onions; cover and simmer for 15 minutes or until the sauce has thickened a little and the meat is tender.

SPICY BEEF STEW II

SERVES 4

1 kg/2 lb stewing beef, cut into 5 cm/2 in cubes
2 stalks lemon grass, sliced paper-thin and finely chopped
2 fresh red chillies, minced
2 tsp sugar
2 tbsp fresh ginger, grated
2 tsp ground cinnamon
2 tsp curry powder
45 ml/3 tbsp Nuoc Mam sauce or 45 ml/3 tbsp light soya sauce and 3 ml/½ tsp anchovy essence
salt and freshly ground black pepper

65 ml/4½ tbsp vegetable oil
1 large onion, minced
6 cloves garlic, minced
100 ml/4 fl oz tomato purée
4 star anise
1.2 litres/2 pt water
2 medium carrots, cut into 2.5 cm/1 in chunks
2 medium potatoes, peeled and cut into 2.5 cm/1 in chunks
1 small daikon (white Chinese radish), peeled and cut into 2.5 cm/1 in chunks

◆ Mix the beef, lemon grass, chillies, sugar, ginger, cinnamon, curry powder, Nuoc Mam sauce, salt and black pepper and leave to stand for 1 hour.

◆ Heat 60 ml/4 tbsp oil in the wok over a high heat. Add the beef and marinade and stir quickly to sear. Remove and set aside.

◆ Add a little more oil and, when hot, add the onion and garlic and stir-fry until fragrant. Add the tomato purée and stir for 2 minutes. Add the beef, star anise, a little salt and the water. Bring the mixture to the boil, reduce the heat, cover and simmer until the beef is tender.

◆ Add the carrots and simmer for 10 minutes. Add the potatoes and simmer for a further 10 minutes. Finally, add the daikon and cook for another 10 minutes.

MEXICAN

BISTEK RANCHERO

SERVES 2

350 g/12 oz steak, thinly sliced
10 ml/2 tsp olive oil
salt and pepper
½ onion, thickly sliced
1 large tomato

1 large green chilli, sliced into "wheels"
2 chopped serrano chillies
30 ml/2 tbsp chicken stock

◆ Fry the meat in the oil with the salt and pepper. When it is almost done, add the other ingredients and stir to coat the meat thoroughly. Cover, and cook well.

◆ Serve with refried beans.

Above: Spicy Beef Stew

PORK WITH MUSSELS

This is one of several Spanish dishes called mar y muntanya *– sea and mountain. At first this was an economical way of eking out small quantities – almost like a starter and a main course put together to make one dish for 8 people! Later, simple mixtures like this one became more lavish, with combinations like chicken and lobster.*

SERVES 8

25 g/1 oz lard
850 g/1¾ lb lean pork, cubed
salt and freshly ground black pepper
30 ml/2 tbsp olive oil
750 ml/1½ lb onions, chopped
6 garlic cloves, finely chopped
800 g/1 lb 12 oz can tomatoes
1 tbsp paprika
½ dried chilli, seeded and chopped,
   or a pinch of cayenne pepper

2 bay leaves
1 strip of dried orange peel or
   2 strips of fresh zest
1.5 kg/3 lb mussels, cleaned
200 ml/7 fl oz dry white wine
6 tbsp chopped fresh parsley

◆ Heat the lard in a large casserole, season the pork well and fry until it is golden on all sides. Remove from the pan.

◆ Add the oil and chopped onions and cook gently until soft. Add the garlic, tomatoes (breaking them up with a spoon), paprika, chilli or cayenne pepper, bay leaves and orange peel or zest and cook for 20 minutes until reduced.

◆ Meanwhile open the mussels in a big saucepan. Put in the wine and 2 tablespoons of parsley. Add half the shellfish and cover tightly. Steam for 4 minutes, shaking the pan occasionally if they are not all in one layer. Remove the first batch of mussels from the pan and cook the second batch.

◆ Remove the top shells from each mussel and throw away any mussels that smell strongly or that remain obstinately shut.

◆ Add the pork and the mussel liquor to the sauce and simmer for 30 minutes, until the meat is tender and the sauce has reduced. Check the seasoning, add the mussels and warm through. Sprinkle with parsley and serve.

STEAMED GROUND RICE-PORK WRAPPED IN LOTUS LEAVES

SERVES 6–7

3–4 lotus leaves
750 g/1½ lb belly of pork, thick end
30 ml/2 tbsp light soya sauce
vegetable oil for deep-frying
2 slices fresh root ginger
2 spring onions

22 ml/1½ tbsp oyster sauce
½ tsp salt
1½ tsp sugar
2 cloves garlic
3 tbsp ground rice
7 ml/1½ tsp sesame seed oil

◆ Immerse the lotus leaves in warm water for 3–4 minutes to soften. Bring a large pan of water to the boil, add the pork and simmer for 10 minutes. Remove and drain. Rub the pork with the soya sauce. Heat the oil in a wok or deep-fryer. When hot, fry the pork for about 3 minutes. Drain. Cut the pork into 1 cm/½ in slices.

◆ Finely chop the ginger and spring onions. Mix together the oyster sauce, salt, sugar, ginger, garlic and spring onions. Add the ground rice and sesame seed oil. Mix in the pork slices and make sure they are evenly coated. Pile the slices neatly into a stack, then wrap in the softened lotus leaves. Tie securely with string.

◆ Place the parcel in a heatproof dish, put in a steamer and steam for 3 hours. When ready, drain away any excess water and serve straight from the lotus leaves. The pork will be tender and the ground rice will have soaked up any fattiness.

STIR-FRIED PORK SLICES WITH FRESH VEGETABLES

SERVES 4–6

225 g/8 oz pork fillet
15 ml/1 tbsp soya sauce
1 tbsp rice wine or dry sherry
1 tsp sugar
½ tbsp cornflour

225 g/8 oz fresh mushrooms
1 small Chinese cabbage
1 spring onion
45 ml/3 tbsp oil
1 tsp salt

◆ Heat up about 15 ml/1 tbsp of oil; before it gets too hot, stir-fry the pork for about 1 minute or until the colour of the meat changes; then dish out and keep it aside.

◆ Wash and dry the wok; heat up the remaining oil. When it smokes, toss in the finely chopped onion followed by the mushrooms and cabbage; add salt and stir constantly for about ½ minute, then return the pork to the wok and mix it well with the vegetables; add a little stock or water if necessary. As soon as the gravy starts to bubble it is ready to serve.

◆ Cut the pork into small slices, about the size of an oblong stamp; mix with soya sauce, rice wine or sherry, sugar and cornflour. Wash the mushrooms and cut them into thin slices. Cut the cabbage into pieces about the same size as the pork. Finely chop the onion.

ROAST PORK WITH APPLE-WALNUT STUFFING

As elegant as it looks, this stuffed roast is not difficult to make. The most important tools are string to retie the roast after stuffing, a meat thermometer to determine when it is cooked through and a sharp carving knife. The stuffing is delicious – tart apples complemented by sautéed onions, the sweetness of sultanas, the crunch of walnuts, and just a touch of cloves for spiciness. You may want to make some extra stuffing to serve on the side. The walnut halves should be cut into 2–4 pieces each, but not chopped any smaller. If the sultanas are dry, soak in hot water for 20 minutes, then drain. You may substitute raisins, if necessary, but the sweetness is not the same.
The roast is easiest to handle in one piece. However, if the roast is cut in half, you can still stuff it and tie it back together – it's just a little messier.

SERVES 8

75 g/3 oz butter, divided	125 g/4 oz walnut pieces
2 large Pippin or other tart apples,	75 g/3 oz sultanas
peeled, cored and cut into	½ tsp salt
1 cm/½-in chunks	¼ tsp ground cloves
1 small onion, chopped	½ tsp dry mustard
2 sticks celery, chopped	1 boned pork loin roast,
1 clove garlic, finely chopped	1.5–1.6 kg/3–3½ lb
175 g/6 oz soft breadcrumbs	30–45 ml/2–3 tbsp vegetable oil

◆ In a medium frying pan, melt 40 g/1½ oz butter. Sauté the apples until barely tender, 7–10 minutes. Remove the apples and set aside.

◆ Add 40 g/1½ oz butter to the frying pan and sauté the onion, celery and garlic until the onion is limp, about 5 minutes. Set aside.

◆ In a large bowl, combine the apples, sautéed vegetables, breadcrumbs, walnuts, sultanas, salt, cloves and dry mustard. This stuffing is not intended to adhere in a solid mass, but it should be moist. If the pan juices are not sufficient, add a little milk. Set the stuffing aside.

◆ Cut the pork almost in half along its length. Spread it out and make lengthwise slashes along its thickest parts. If it is already cut in half, make 1 or 2 lengthwise slashes in each half.

◆ Preheat the oven to 190°C/375°F/Gas Mark 5. In a large frying pan, heat the oil. Briefly cook the pork until the outside is browned, then remove from the pan. Set on a flat surface and spread it out with 4–6 lengths of kitchen string underneath. Mound the stuffing into the slashes. Carefully bring up the sides of the roast and tightly tie into a roll. If the stuffing falls out while you are reshaping the roast, just stuff it back in.

◆ Place the retied roast on a rack in a roasting tin. Roast until a thermometer inserted in the thickest part of the meat (but not inserted so far that it is measuring the temperature of the stuffing rather than the meat) registers at least 65°C/150°F. This reading gives a very moist and slightly pink pork, and is hot enough to kill any trichinosis parasites. You may cook to 75°C/165°F if you prefer well-done pork. To estimate cooking time, figure 25–30 minutes per 450 g/1 lb, but rely on the thermometer to tell you when it is done.

◆ Remove the roast from the oven and let it sit for 15 minutes before carving.

NOTE: If there is any leftover stuffing, or if you have made extra, put it in a lightly buttered casserole dish and cook for 15–25 minutes (depending on quantity) at 190°C/375°F/Gas Mark 5.

QUICK-FRIED SHREDDED PORK IN CAPITAL SAUCE

SERVES 4–6

350 g/12 oz pork fillet
½ tsp salt
20 g/¾ oz cornflour
1 egg white
2 spring onions
vegetable oil for deep-frying

Capital Sauce
45 ml/3 tbsp vegetable oil

22 ml/1½ tsp yellow bean paste
15 g/½ oz sugar
7 ml/½ tbsp dark soya sauce
15 ml/1 tbsp rice wine or dry sherry
½ tbsp cornflour blended with
    30 ml/2 tbsp water
5 ml/1 tsp sesame seed oil

◆ Cut the pork into matchsticks. Mix with the salt, cornflour and egg white. Cut the spring onion into 1 cm/½ in sections.

◆ Heat the oil in a wok or deep-fryer. When hot, add the pork, separating all the shreds, and stir-fry for about 2 minutes. Drain and pour off the oil to use for other purposes.

◆ Meanwhile, heat the 45 ml/3 tbsp of oil in a wok or pan. When hot, add the yellow bean paste, sugar, soya sauce and rice wine or sherry. Stir until smooth and glossy, then stir in the blended cornflour. Bring back to the boil and add the pork. Stir in the spring onions and sprinkle over the sesame seed oil.

◆ Serve on crispy rice-flour noodles. If liked, wrap spoonfuls of pork and rice in lettuce leaves to eat with the fingers.

PORK VINDALOO

SERVES 4

6 cloves garlic
25 g/1 oz fresh ginger
4 red chillies, seeded
1 tsp mustard seeds
½ tsp fenugreek seeds
½ tsp turmeric
½ tsp ground cumin
60 ml/4 tbsp white wine vinegar
30–45 ml/2–3 tbsp oil
2 onions, finely chopped

225 g/8 oz tomatoes, peeled and
 chopped
1–1.4 kg/2–3 lb shoulder of pork,
 trimmed and cubed
salt
600 ml/1 pt boiling water
4–6 curry leaves
6 cloves
2.5 cm/1 in cinnamon stick
1 tsp sugar

◆ Chop 4 cloves garlic with half the ginger, then grind, pound or blend in a liquidizer with the chillies, mustard seeds, fenugreek seeds, turmeric and half the vinegar.

◆ Heat the oil, add the onion and fry until golden.

◆ Add the spice paste, stir and fry gently for 15 minutes.

◆ Add the tomato and continue to cook, mashing it under the back of a wooden spoon to make a paste.

◆ When the oil has run clear of the spices, add the pork and fry for 5 minutes, turning the pieces in the spice mixture.

◆ Add ½ tsp salt and pour on the boiling water. Simmer, covered, for 40 minutes, until the pork is tender.

◆ Slice the remaining garlic and ginger and add with the curry leaves, cloves and cinnamon stick. Cook for a further 5 minutes.

◆ Add the sugar and remaining vinegar. Add salt to taste.

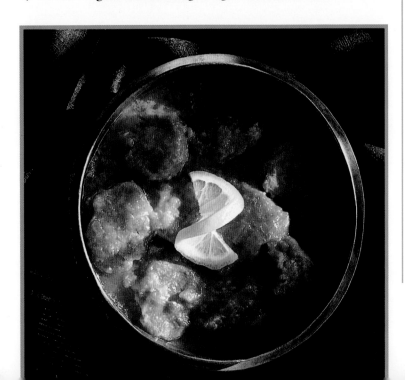

SICHUAN YU-HSIANG SHREDDED PORK

SERVES 4–6

225 g/8 oz pork fillet
2 spring onions
2 slices fresh root ginger
2 fresh chillies
1 clove garlic, crushed
3–4 dried Chinese mushrooms
25 g/1 oz canned bamboo shoots,
 drained
2 egg whites
2 tsp cornflour
vegetable oil for deep-frying
½ tsp salt
15 ml/1 tbsp yellow bean paste

15 ml/1 tbsp good stock (see p.12)
15 ml/1 tbsp rice wine or dry sherry
22 ml/1½ tbsp soya sauce
22 ml/1½ tbsp vinegar
½ tsp white pepper
2 tsp cornflour blended with 30 ml/
 2 tbsp cold stock
5 ml/1 tsp sesame seed oil
2 tsp red chilli oil or chilli sauce
1 tsp crushed Sichuan peppercorns

◆ Shred the pork fillet finely. Chop the spring onions, ginger, chillies, discarding the seeds, and garlic. Soak the dried mushrooms in boiling water to cover for 25 minutes. Drain and discard the tough stalks. Shred the mushroom caps. Shred the bamboo shoots.

◆ Put the pork in a bowl with the egg whites, cornflour and 15 ml/1 tbsp oil. Toss together very well.

◆ Heat the oil in a wok or deep-fryer. When medium hot, fry the pork for about 1½ minutes. Add the bamboo shoots and mushrooms and stir for about 1½ minutes. Drain and pour away the oil. Reheat the wok or a pan with about 15 ml/1 tbsp of oil. When hot, stir-fry the ginger, garlic, spring onions, salt and chillies for 1 minute. Add the yellow bean paste, stock, sherry or wine, soya sauce, vinegar and white pepper. Stir and bring to the boil.

◆ Add the shredded pork and vegetables to the wok. Thicken the sauce with the blended cornflour. At the last minute, drizzle over the sesame seed oil and toss together. Transfer to a heated plate and sprinkle on the red chilli oil and crushed peppercorns.

SPICY GRILLED PORK ON A BED OF VERMICELLI

SERVES 4

225 g/8 oz rice vermicelli
450 g/1 lb fresh belly pork with skin,
    cut against the grain into 8 mm/¼
    in strips, about 5 cm/2 in long
450 g/1 lb beef, minced
8 cloves garlic, minced

Caramel Sauce
100 g/4 oz sugar
50 ml/2 fl oz Nuoc Mam sauce, or
    Maggi sauce and ½ tsp anchovy
    essence, mixed thoroughly
4 spring onions, thinly sliced
freshly ground black pepper

◆ Soak the vermicelli in warm water until soft. Drain and set aside.

◆ Make the caramel sauce by swirling the sugar gently in a wok over a hot heat. Be careful not to let the sugar blacken but ignore the smoke. Remove from the heat and add the Nuoc Mam sauce or Maggi substitute. Return to a low heat and gently boil until the sugar dissolves. Add the spring onions and pepper and stir.

◆ Put 24 bamboo skewers into water and allow to soak for at least 30 minutes.

◆ Meanwhile, put the pork and beef into two separate bowls. Put the garlic and half of the caramel sauce onto the beef. Put the remainder of the caramel sauce onto the pork. Blend both with the hand and allow to stand for 30 minutes. Make 24 meatballs out of the beef.

◆ Skewer the beef balls and pork slices and cook under a hot grill for 15–20 minutes, turning frequently. Place on the bed of vermicelli to serve.

Above: Deep-Fried Crispy Fingers of Pork

DEEP-FRIED CRISPY FINGERS OF PORK

SERVES 5–6

750 g/1½ lb lean pork
1 tsp salt
¼ tsp pepper
½ tsp ground ginger
15 ml/1 tbsp rice wine or dry sherry
5 ml/1 tsp sesame seed oil
vegetable oil for deep-frying

Batter
1 egg
30 g/1¼ oz plain flour
20 g/¾ oz cornflour

Sauce
22 ml/1½ tbsp vegetable oil

1½ tbsp spring onion, chopped
2 tsp garlic, crushed
2 tsp fresh chillies, chopped
1½ tbsp fresh root ginger, chopped
75 ml/5 tbsp good stock (see p.12)
30 ml/2 tbsp vinegar
30 ml/2 tbsp light soya sauce
1 tsp salt
1 tsp sugar

To garnish
radish rose
halved lemon slices

◆ Cut the pork into finger-sized strips. Mix the salt, pepper, ginger, wine or sherry and sesame seed oil together. Add the pork and mix thoroughly. Leave to marinate for 10 minutes.
◆ To make the batter, mix the egg, flour and cornflour together.
◆ To make the dip sauce, heat the oil in a wok or pan. When hot, add the onion, garlic, chilli and ginger and stir for a few seconds. Add the rest of the dip sauce ingredients. Bring to the boil, then pour into a small heatproof bowl.
◆ Heat the oil in a wok or deep-fryer. When very hot, dip the pork fingers in the batter and put gently into the oil. Fry for about 3 minutes. Drain. Allow the oil to reheat, then fry the pork again for 30 seconds. Drain. Arrange the pork fingers on a heated plate and serve with the dip sauce.

ANTS CLIMBING TREES

The ground pork forms the "ants", the transparent noodles the "trees".

SERVES 4–6

225 g/8 oz pork
30 ml/2 tbsp soya sauce
15 g/½ oz sugar
1 tsp cornflour
½ tsp chilli paste

125 g/4 oz transparent noodles
45 ml/3 tbsp oil
1 small red chilli
2 spring onions, chopped
150 ml/¼ pt stock or water

◆ Mince the pork; mix it with the soya sauce, sugar, cornflour and chilli paste. Soak the noodles in warm water for 10 minutes.
◆ Heat up the oil; first fry the chilli and onions, then the pork. When the colour of the meat starts to change, drain the noodles and add them to the pan. Blend well, then add the stock or water; continue cooking. When all the liquid is absorbed, the dish is ready to serve.

67

SWEET AND SOUR SPARERIBS

SERVES 4–6

450 g/1 lb pork spareribs
30 ml/2 tbsp soya sauce
15 ml/1 tbsp rice wine or dry sherry
½ tsp monosodium glutamate
15 g/½ oz cornflour

25 g/1 oz sugar
22 ml/1½ tbsp vinegar
lard for deep-frying
salt and Sichuan pepper for dipping

◆ Chop the spareribs into small bits, using a cleaver. Mix 7 ml/½ tbsp of soya sauce with the rice wine or sherry and monosodium glutamate. When they are all well blended together, add half the cornflour. Coat each bit of the sparerib with this mixture.

◆ In a bowl, mix the remaining soya sauce with sugar and vinegar. Warm up the lard in a wok or deep-fryer, put in about half of the spareribs, fry for 30 seconds, then scoop them out. Wait for a while to let the lard heat up again, then fry the rest of the spareribs for 30 seconds and scoop out. Now wait for the lard to get hot before returning all the spareribs to the wok to fry for another 50 seconds or so; scoop them out when they turn golden and place them on a serving dish.

◆ Pour off the excess lard, leaving about 1 tbsp in the pan; add the sauce mixture. When it starts to bubble, add the remaining cornflour mixed in a little cold water; stir to make a smooth sauce, then pour it over the spareribs.

◆ Serve with salt and pepper mixed as a dip.

CITRUSY PORK FILLET
WITH MANGO-PAPAYA CHUTNEY

SERVES 4–6

100 ml/4 fl oz fresh orange juice
15 ml/1 tbsp fresh lime juice
1½ tsp sugar
½ tsp salt
¼ tsp ground allspice
pinch of ground nutmeg
1 tsp grated root ginger
3 cloves garlic, minced
225 g/8 oz pork fillet
vegetable oil
½ tsp demerara sugar

Mango-Papaya Chutney
1 ripe mango or 125 g/4 oz canned
    unsweetened mango, cut into
    bite-sized chunks
1 ripe papaya or 2 nectarines or
    75 g/3 oz canned unsweetened
    papaya, cut into bite-sized
    chunks
1 tbsp chopped spring onions
15 ml/1 tbsp fresh lime juice
1 tbsp chopped fresh coriander
1 tsp chopped hot pepper or hot
    pepper sauce

◆ Combine the orange juice, lime juice, sugar, salt, allspice, nutmeg, ginger and garlic in a large sealable plastic food storage bag. Add the pork, seal the bag, and marinate in the refrigerator for 8 hours, turning occasionally.

◆ Preheat the oven to 180°C/350°F/Gas Mark 4. Remove the pork from the bag, reserving the marinade. Place the pork on a rack brushed with oil. Place the rack in a shallow roasting tin and pour hot water and half the reserved marinade into the roasting tin to a depth of 1 cm/½ in. Insert a meat thermometer into the thickest part of the pork. Bake for 40 minutes, or until the meat thermometer registers 71°C/160°F, basting frequently with the remaining marinade mixed with demerara sugar.

◆ While the meat is cooking, combine the mango, papaya, spring onions, lime juice, coriander and hot pepper or hot pepper sauce. Chill and serve with the pork.

PORK WITH CABBAGE AND CORN

*A modern Mexican would probably make this with a can of
corn. Frozen corn is good, too, but for the very best flavour you
need to scrape the corn from 2 or 3 fresh ears.*

SERVES 6

750 g/1½ lb pork ribs, chopped	8 peppercorns
1 medium onion, cut in rings	30 ml/2 tbsp vinegar
2 large tomatoes, cut in rings	1 medium cabbage, sliced
2 cloves garlic	350 g/12 oz sweet corn
pinch of cumin seed	salt and pepper

◆ Using a heavy flameproof casserole, cook the pork in just enough
water to cover. When the ribs are tender (at least an hour), add the
onion and the tomato. Cook for a few minutes longer.

◆ In a blender, combine the garlic, the cumin, the peppercorns
and the vinegar. Add to the meat, together with the cabbage and
corn. Stir well and season: the meal is ready when the cabbage is
cooked. Serve with boiled rice.

Poultry

*T**he Orient has a hundred ways with poultry, in Spain, Greece and the Lebanon it is served with olives, almonds and apricots, while in the Caribbean it is jazzed up with rum and coconut.***

GRILLED CHICKEN

SERVES 4

1 kg/2 lb boned chicken thigh
4 young leeks, washed and trimmed

Yakitori Sauce
450 ml/¾ pt dark soya sauce

200 ml/7 fl oz chicken stock
200 ml/7 fl oz sake
125 g/4 oz sugar
100 ml/3½ fl oz mirin

◆ Combine the yakitori sauce ingredients in a saucepan. Bring to the boil and simmer gently for 5 minutes. Remove from the heat and cool to room temperature. Transfer the sauce to a deep jar.

◆ Cut the chicken into 25 cm/1 in pieces, and cut the leeks into 4 cm/1½ in lengths. Thread the chicken and leeks alternately onto bamboo skewers.

◆ Grill over the hottest flame, turning frequently to avoid burning. When the juices begin to drip, dip the skewered chicken into the sauce and return to the grill. Repeat this several times until the chicken is lightly cooked. Be careful not to overcook the chicken; it should remain moist.

◆ Serve the chicken piping hot, on the skewers, and spoon over a little of the yakitori sauce. Traditionally, yakitori is sprinkled with a little dash of seven-spice pepper, and eaten with the fingers straight from the skewer.

CHICKEN BRAISED WITH BACON AND RED PEPPERS

SERVES 4

1 roasting chicken (about 1.25 kg/ 2½ lb)	4 cloves garlic
	4 chilli peppers
60 ml/4 tbsp olive oil	225 g/8 oz bacon or *pancetta*
4 red sweet peppers	salt

◆ Joint the chicken into 4 pieces. Heat the oil in your heaviest casserole – one with a good lid – and thoroughly brown the chicken pieces. Remove them from the heat.

◆ Deseed the red peppers and slice into fine strips. Cook until soft in the chicken oil – about 10 minutes. Return the chicken pieces to the pan, smothering them with the peppers.

◆ Add the whole garlic and the whole chillies. Lay the strips of bacon over everything, cover the pan and cook at a very low heat until the chicken is tender – about 30 minutes.

◆ Season lightly with the salt. (Remember that with the bacon, you will need little.)

CARIBBEAN COCONUT CHICKEN

SERVES 4

4 chicken breasts, halved, boned, skinned and fat cut off
30 ml/2 tbsp vegetable oil
1 large red sweet pepper, cored, seeded and diced
1 large green sweet pepper, cored, seeded and diced
1 large onion, chopped
1 clove garlic, crushed
50 g/2 oz unsweetened coconut flakes, toasted

2 tsp grated lime rind
salt
25 g/1 oz butter or margine
¼ tsp sweet paprika
¼ tsp hot pepper sauce
15 ml/1 tbsp lime juice
1 tbsp apricot preserve
fresh coriander, to garnish (optional)

◆ Preheat the oven to 180°/350°F/Gas Mark 4. Pound the chicken to 8 mm/¼ in thickness between two sheets of clingfilm and set aside. Heat the oil to medium hot in a large frying pan and fry the peppers, onion and garlic for about 10 minutes, stirring frequently, until slightly soft. Remove from the heat. In the same pan, stir in the coconut, lime rind and salt to taste.

◆ Spoon one-eighth of vegetable mixture over the centre of each chicken breast. Bring the long ends of each breast up over the filling and secure with cocktail sticks. Place the butter or margarine in a small roasting tin and melt over medium heat. Place the chicken rolls, seam-side down, in the tin. In a small bowl, combine the paprika, hot pepper sauce and ½ tsp salt and sprinkle the mixture over the chicken rolls. Bake for 25–30 minutes until the chicken is cooked through and juices run clear when the roll is pierced with a knife. Remove the rolls to a chopping board.

◆ Stir the lime juice and apricot preserve into the drippings in the roasting tin and bring to the boil, stirring to loosen browned bits on the bottom of the tin and to blend. Remove from the heat.

◆ Remove the cocktail sticks from the chicken rolls and cut into 1 cm/½ in slices. Arrange the slices on a serving dish and pour the sauce over. Garnish with fresh coriander if desired.

JAPANESE

DEEP-FRIED CHICKEN TATSUTA STYLE

SERVES 4

750 g/1½ lb boned chicken, skin attached
40 g/1½ oz cornflour
vegetable oil for deep-frying
1 lemon, washed, dried and quartered
4 sprigs of parsley, washed and patted dry

Marinade
60 ml/4 tbsp soy sauce
30 ml/2 tbsp sake
1 tbsp sugar
15 ml/1 tbsp ginger juice (see p.9)

◆ Cut the chicken into large bite-sized chunks. Mix the marinade ingredients and pour over the chicken. Mix well so that the chicken is evenly covered. Set aside to marinate for 30 minutes.

◆ Drain the chicken and coat with cornflour. Wait for a few minutes so that the coating can set.

◆ In a small saucepan, heat oil for deep-frying to 180°C/350°F. Carefully place the chicken in the oil, a few pieces at a time, and deep-fry for about 3 minutes, until crisp and brown.

◆ Remove piece by piece and drain. Arrange a few pieces of chicken on a neatly folded napkin. Garnish with lemon quarters and sprigs of parsley.

GREEK

CHICKEN WITH FETA AND GREEN OLIVES

This dish originates from a small village called Barthouna, near Sparta. It is either prepared with olives or raisins, both being major products of this region.

SERVES 4

4 chicken breasts
flour, for dredging
salt and freshly ground black
   pepper, to taste
90 ml/6 tbsp olive oil
350 g/12 oz button onions (or use
   large onions, quartered)

400 g/14 oz can chopped tomatoes
120 ml/4 fl oz boiling water
275 g/10 oz pitted green olives,
   washed and drained
15 ml/1 tbsp red wine vinegar
125 g/4 oz feta cheese, thinly sliced

◆ Arrange the chicken breasts on a chopping board, dredge with the flour and season with salt and freshly ground black pepper on both sides.

◆ Heat the oil in a large, deep frying pan and add the chicken breasts, skin-side down. Cook on both sides for 3–5 minutes or until browned. Lift the chicken breasts out of the pan and set aside.

◆ Add the onions to the frying pan and sauté for about 5 minutes or until softened, stirring frequently. Return the chicken to the pan and add the chopped tomatoes and boiling water. Season with salt and freshly ground black pepper, cover, and simmer for 25–30 minutes or until the chicken is tender and cooked through, adding a little extra boiling water if necessary.

◆ In the last 10 minutes of the cooking time, add the green olives and red wine vinegar. Stir to combine. Place a slice of feta cheese on top of each piece of chicken and continue to cook, uncovered, for a further 10 minutes, or until the feta cheese has just melted. Serve immediately.

POACHED CHICKEN WITH MELON

*T*his unusual and refreshing chilled dish looks pretty when
served with wild rice. You might want to serve this on chilled
plates; glass or crystal are perfect.

SERVES 4

375 ml/12 fl oz chicken stock
4 skinned, boneless chicken breasts,
    trimmed of fat
45 ml/3 tbsp red wine vinegar
15 g/½ oz dark brown sugar
2 cloves garlic, minced
1 tsp minced fresh root ginger

1 tsp Dijon mustard
75 g/3 oz diced mango
50 g/2 oz orange-flesh melon balls
50 g/2 oz cantaloupe balls
freshly-snipped chives to garnish
    (optional)

◆ In a medium-sized frying pan, bring stock to a boil, then reduce the heat to low and simmer. Add the chicken, cover and simmer until cooked through and the juices run clear, 8–10 minutes. With a slotted spatula, remove the chicken from the frying pan. Leave to cool, then cover and refrigerate until chilled, about 2 hours.

◆ Meanwhile, boil the stock until it is reduced to 125 ml/4 fl oz. Stir in the remaining ingredients except the mango and melon balls and cook, stirring frequently, for 5 minutes. Gently stir in the mango and melon balls. Toss to coat. Refrigerate for 2 hours until chilled. Garnish with snipped chives and serve.

SWEET SOUR 'N' HOT CHICKEN

SERVES 4

175 g/6 oz marmalade
100 ml/4 fl oz lime juice
1 tsp chopped root ginger
1 tsp ground nutmeg
dash of hot pepper sauce
15 ml/1 tbsp vegetable oil
4 large chicken breasts (about
    750 g/1½ lb), boned, skinned, fat
    cut off, cut into 2.5 cm/1 in cubes

1 medium papaya, seeded, halved
    and cut into 2.5 cm/1 in cubes
175 g/6 oz can sliced water
    chestnuts, drained
15 g/½ oz fresh coriander, chopped

◆ In a small saucepan, melt the marmalade over a low heat, gradually blending in the lime juice, ginger, nutmeg and hot pepper sauce. Heat the oil in a frying pan and brown the chicken cubes. Add the papaya and toss for several minutes, then add the sauce and water chestnuts. Cook over a moderate heat for about 3–4 minutes until the chicken is cooked. Taste the sauce and add hot pepper sauce to taste. Place on a serving dish and sprinkle with coriander.

CHICKEN IN "BIRD'S NEST"

SERVES 4–6

225 g/8 oz potatoes
½ tbsp salt
30 g/1¼ oz cornflour
oil for deep-frying
1 lettuce heart
225 g/8 oz chicken breast meat,
    boned

1 egg white
225 g/8 oz celery
2 spring onions
1 slice fresh root ginger
7 ml/½ tbsp rice wine or dry sherry

◆ Cut the potatoes into thin shreds; wash and rinse in cold water, drain and dry. Mix with a little salt and 15/½ oz cornflour. Arrange the shreds in a criss-cross pattern against the side of a strainer, then place another strainer on top of it. Submerge both in hot oil and deep-fry for about 4 minutes until golden. This is the "bird's nest".

◆ Drain and take the "bird's nest" out of the strainer and place it in a serving dish on a bed of lettuce heart.

◆ Shred the chicken breast meat. Marinate in a little salt, egg white and cornflour. Shred the celery to the same size as the chicken. Finely chop the onions and root ginger.

◆ Warm up about 30 ml/2 tbsp of oil; stir-fry the chicken meat for about 1 minute, remove: heat up a little more oil, toss in the onions and root ginger, followed by the celery. Add salt and rice wine or sherry, stir a few times then add the chicken meat; cook together for about another minute, place it in the "bird's nest" and serve.

JAPANESE

SWEET GLAZED CHICKEN

SERVES 4

2 chicken legs and thighs, boned	teriyaki sauce
vegetable oil	

◆ Pierce the skin of the chicken with a fork to allow the sauce to penetrate. Brush a frying pan with oil and fry the chicken over high heat, turning, until well browned.

◆ Remove the chicken from the heat and rinse with boiling water. Return the chicken pieces to the pan and pour over the teriyaki sauce. Cook until the sauce is glossy, turning the chicken so that it is well coated in sauce. Remove from the heat when the sauce is well reduced and thick.

◆ Cut the chicken into 2 cm/½ in slices, and arrange the slices on individual plates. Serve hot.

POLISH

ROAST CHICKEN WITH BUCKWHEAT

If you would prefer to stuff the chicken with a breadcrumb mixture, try the dill stuffing described in the note at the end.

SERVES 4–6

175 g/6 oz roasted buckwheat	125 g/4 oz chicken livers, chopped
475 ml/16 fl oz water	½ tsp dried marjoram
1 onion, finely chopped	salt and freshly ground black pepper
25 g/1 oz butter	1 egg, beaten
1 clove garlic, crushed (optional)	1.5 kg/3½ lb chicken

◆ Place the buckwheat in a sieve and rinse under cold running water. Put the buckwheat in a saucepan and pour in the water. Heat very gently until the water is just about simmering. Remove the pan from the heat, cover and leave for 30 minutes, by which time the buckwheat should have absorbed all the water.

◆ Cook the onion in the butter for 10 minutes, until soft but not browned. Add the garlic and chicken livers and cook for a further 5 minutes, stirring occasionally, until the pieces of liver are firm. Add this mixture to the buckwheat with the marjoram and seasoning to taste. Stir in the egg to bind, making sure all the ingredients are thoroughly combined.

◆ Preheat the oven to 180°C/350°F/Gas Mark 4. Rinse the chicken under cold running water, drain well and pat dry with absorbent kitchen paper. Spoon the stuffing into the body cavity and truss the bird neatly, tying string around the legs and wings. Place in a roasting tin. Roast for 1¾ hours, or until the chicken is golden, crisp and cooked through. Halfway through cooking, pour a little water into the bottom of the roasting tin and keep topping this up as it evaporates.

◆ Transfer the cooked chicken to a warmed serving plate. Add a little extra water to the cooking juices, if necessary, and boil the liquid, scraping all the roasting residue off the pan. When the gravy is reduced and flavoursome, check the seasoning and serve a little poured over the chicken.

> NOTE: To make a dill stuffing, cook 1 small onion in 25 g/1 oz butter until soft. Mix the onion with 175 g/6 oz fresh white breadcrumbs, 4 tbsp chopped fresh dill, salt and freshly ground black pepper and 2 egg yolks. Whisk the egg whites until they peak softly, then stir into the stuffing.

CARIBBEAN

STEWED CHICKEN TRINIDAD-STYLE

SERVES 4–6

30 ml/2 tbsp lime juice
1 medium onion, chopped
1 large tomato, cut into 8 wedges
1 celery stick, chopped
1 tbsp chopped spring onion
3 tbsp minced fresh coriander
1 clove garlic, chopped
⅛ tsp dried thyme, crumbled
1 tsp salt
⅛ tsp freshly ground black pepper
1 tbsp white wine vinegar
30 ml/2 tbsp Worcestershire sauce

750g–1 kg/1½–2 lb chicken, cut into
   serving pieces
30 ml/2 tbsp vegetable oil
25 g/1 oz dark brown sugar
30 ml/2 tbsp tomato ketchup
225 ml/8 fl oz water
225 g/8 oz cabbage, shredded
   (optional)

To garnish
celery leaves (optional)
lime slices (optional)

◆ In a large bowl, combine the lime juice, onion, tomato, celery, spring onion, coriander, garlic, thyme, salt, pepper, vinegar and Worcestershire sauce. Add the chicken, turning it to coat well, and leave it to marinate in the refrigerator, covered, overnight.

◆ In a heavy-based saucepan, heat the oil over medium-high heat until it is hot but not smoking and add the sugar. When the sugar mixture begins to bubble, transfer the chicken in batches to the pan, using a slotted spoon. Reserve the marinade mixture. Cook the chicken, turning it until it is browned well, and transfer it to absorbent kitchen paper to drain. Stir the reserved marinade mixture, tomato ketchup and water into the fat remaining in the saucepan and return the chicken to the pan. Bring the mixture to a boil and simmer it, covered, stirring occasionally, for 30 minutes. Add the shredded cabbage, if using, and simmer for 15–20 minutes until the thickest pieces of chicken are done. Garnish with celery leaves or lime slices if desired.

SHANGHAI QUICK-BRAISED CHICKEN ON THE BONE

SERVES 6–8

1.5–1.7 kg/3–4 lb chicken	45 ml/3 tbsp dark soya sauce
1 tbsp cornflour	15 ml/1 tbsp hoisin sauce
60 ml/4 tbsp vegetable oil	15 ml/1 tbsp oyster sauce
5 slices fresh root ginger	60 ml/4 tbsp rice wine or dry sherry
25 g/1 oz sugar	450 ml/¾ pt good stock (see p. 12)
45 ml/3 tbsp light soya sauce	spring onions

◆ Chop the chicken through the bone into about 30 bite-sized pieces. Bring a large pan of water to the boil, add the chicken and simmer for about 5 minutes. Remove and drain thoroughly. Blend the cornflour with 45 ml/3 tbsp of water.

◆ Heat the oil in a wok or pan. When hot, stir in the ginger for about 1½ minutes. Add the chicken pieces and stir-fry for about 3 minutes. Put in the sugar, soya sauces, hoisin sauce, oyster sauce, wine or sherry and stock. Bring to the boil and continue to stir over the highest heat until the sauce begins to thicken and reduce. Add the blended cornflour and stir until the sauce is thick and coats the chicken pieces. Garnish with chopped spring onions.

CHICKEN OREGANO

This simple, tasty dish is perfect for the barbecue on a hot summer's day, or grilled for a fast meze dish.

SERVES 6–8

6–8 chicken portions	salt and freshly ground black
120 ml/4 fl oz olive oil	pepper, to taste
120 ml/4 fl oz dry white wine	2 garlic cloves, crushed
2 tbsp dried oregano	

◆ Arrange the chicken portions in a large, shallow dish.

◆ In a small bowl, combine the oil, wine, oregano, salt and freshly ground black pepper and the garlic. Mix well. Spread the marinade over the chicken portions, cover, and marinate for 2–3 hours, turning and rearranging occasionally.

◆ Place the chicken portions on an oiled grill rack and cook under a preheated grill for about 30 minutes or until the chicken is crisp and golden on the outside and cooked through, turning and rearranging several times during cooking. Serve warm or cold.

Above: Chicken Oregano

CHICKEN KIEV

Chicken Kiev has become a familiar dish, stacked frozen and ready-to-heat in supermarkets and frequently appearing on menus, even in pubs. But the real thing bears little resemblance, in appearance or taste, to such orange monstrosities. This recipe has been simplified to take advantage of prepared chicken breasts.

SERVES 6

150 g/6 oz unsalted butter, softened	salt and freshly ground black pepper
grated rind and juice of 1 large lemon	2 small eggs
	175 g/6 oz fresh fine breadcrumbs
3 tbsp freshly chopped tarragon	oil for deep-frying
6 large skinless chicken breast fillets	

◆ Combine the butter, lemon rind and tarragon in a bowl. With a fork, work the mixture until it is thoroughly mixed. Shape into a block, wrap in foil, and chill until hard.

◆ Lay the chicken breasts on a sheet of greaseproof paper. Trim away any bits attached by membrane. Cover the breasts with another sheet of greaseproof paper and pound with a mallet until they are flattened. Season the fillets as desired.

◆ Cut the butter block into 6 pieces and place one piece in the centre of each fillet. Fold the top and edges over, then roll neatly. Tie the roll with thread.

◆ Beat the eggs lightly in a shallow bowl. Spread the breadcrumbs on a large plate. Dip the breast rolls in the egg then coat them in the breadcrumbs, pressing into the crumbs to make sure they adhere. To obtain a thick "skin" brush the coated rolls with a little more egg if necessary and press into the crumbs again. Place the rolls on a plate and chill for 2–3 hours.

◆ In a deep fryer or heavy saucepan, heat enough oil to cover the breasts completely. When it spits at water droplets (or reaches 190°C/375°F), lower in 3 breasts with a slotted spoon. Fry until golden-brown, about 5–6 minutes. (The oil must not get too hot or the coating will brown before the chicken is cooked.) Drain on absorbent kitchen paper and repeat with the remaining 3 breasts. Serve immediately. Potatoes and cabbage or peas would make a typical accompaniment.

SAKE-STEAMED CHICKEN

SERVES 4

300 g/11 oz boned chicken breast,
   skin attached
1 tbsp salt
30 ml/2 tbsp sake
½ cucumber
4 leaves lettuce
4 lemon wedges

wasabi horseradish, freshly made
   (see p.9)
45 ml/3 tbsp dark soya sauce
ponzu sauce (see p.9)
red maple radish
1 young leek, shredded and rinsed

◆ Put the chicken breast in a bowl, skin side up, and score the skin with a fork. Sprinkle with salt and sake and set aside for 20 minutes to marinate.

◆ Steam the chicken, uncovered, in a preheated steamer over high heat for 15–20 minutes, until just cooked. Allow to cool and slice into 2 cm/¾ in pieces.

◆ Cut the cucumber into 5 cm/2 in lengths, and cut lengthwise into paper-thin slices. Salt lightly, knead, rinse and pat dry.

◆ Wash the lettuce leaves and pat dry. Lay them on 4 small plates. Arrange the chicken slices on the lettuce leaves, and garnish with cucumber slices and lemon wedges.

◆ Prepare the wasabi and serve with soya sauce. Serve with ponzu sauce with red maple radish and shredded leek.

CARAMELIZED CHICKEN WINGS WITH AN ORANGE SAUCE

This dish should have a slightly nutty, burnt flavour, but be careful not to burn the sugar.

SERVES 4

....

8 chicken wings
salt and pepper
30 ml/2 tbsp sesame oil
60 ml/4 tbsp clear honey

60 ml/4 tbsp vegetable oil
25 g/1 oz caster sugar
shredded rind and juice of 1 orange

....

◆ Season the chicken wings with salt and pepper. Mix the sesame oil and honey and spread this over the wings.

◆ Heat the oil in a heavy-based pan and cook the chicken wings for about 4 minutes on each side or until just done. Remove the pan and keep warm. Reserve the pan juices.

◆ Add the sugar to the pan and heat without stirring until it caramelizes. Remove from the heat.

◆ Add the orange juice and reserved pan juices. Stir over a low heat until a smooth sauce forms, adding a little water or orange juice if it becomes too thick. Add half the orange rind and continue to cook over a very low heat.

◆ Place the chicken wings on to a warmed dish. Pour the caramel sauce over them and garnish with the leftover strips of orange.

CHICKEN AND TOMATO CASSEROLE

Kokkinisto *is the name generally given to any meat which is casseroled in a rich tomato sauce.*

SERVES 4–6

50 ml/2 fl oz olive oil	3 garlic cloves, crushed
1.6 kg/3½ lb prepared chicken, cut into portions	salt and freshly ground black pepper, to taste
flour, for dredging	85 ml/3 fl oz boiling water
2 large red onions, sliced	30 ml/2 tbsp red wine vinegar
2 × 400 g/14 oz cans chopped tomatoes	chopped fresh parsley, to garnish

◆ Preheat the oven to 190°C/375°F/Gas Mark 5. Heat the oil in a large, flameproof casserole. Place the chicken portions on a chopping board and dredge all over with flour. Place in the casserole and cook for about 5 minutes, or until evenly browned, turning the portions as they cook. Using a slotted spoon, transfer the chicken portions to a plate and set aside.

◆ Add the onion to the casserole and cook for 3 minutes, or until softened. Return the chicken to the casserole, add the chopped tomatoes and garlic and season with salt and freshly ground black pepper. Add the boiling water, cover the casserole, and cook in the oven for 45–55 minutes or until the chicken is tender and the sauce has thickened.

◆ In the last 5 minutes of cooking time, stir in the red wine vinegar and a little extra boiling water if necessary. Serve sprinkled with chopped fresh parsley.

CHICKEN WITH APRICOTS AND OLIVES

SERVES 8

1.5 kg/3½ lb skinned, boned and cubed chicken	30 ml/2 tbsp lemon juice or white wine vinegar
5 garlic cloves, crushed	120 ml/4 fl oz *arak* (anise-based Lebanese liqueur) or ouzo
150 g/5 oz chopped ready-to-eat dried apricots	2 tsp fresh fennel leaves
50 g/2 oz black Greek olives	22 ml/1½ tbsp olive oil
½ tsp grated orange peel	75 g/3 oz light brown sugar
75 ml/5 tbsp orange juice	

◆ Combine all the ingredients except the sugar in a large bowl and stir carefully to mix well. Cover and chill overnight.

◆ Preheat the oven to 200°C/400°F/Gas Mark 6.

◆ Transfer the chicken pieces to a baking pan and pour over the marinade, including the olives and apricots. Sprinkle over the sugar. Bake for about 30 minutes, turning once or twice.

◆ Remove the chicken pieces to a serving platter, and arrange the olives and apricots over and around them. Strain the cooking juices into a saucepan and reduce over high heat to about half. Pour the sauce over the chicken. Serve warm or cold.

DRUNKEN CHICKEN

SERVES 6–8

1 chicken weighing about 1.5 kg/3 lb
90 ml/6 tbsp soya sauce
45 ml/3 tbsp rice wine or dry sherry
oil for deep-frying
2–3 spring onions, cut to 5 cm/
    2 in lengths

1 tsp salt
150 ml/¼ pt Chinese red wine, or
    port
1.8 litres/3 pt chicken stock

◆ Clean and dry the chicken. Mix 30 ml/2 tbsp each of soya sauce and rice wine or sherry and pour it all over the chicken both inside and out.

◆ Heat up the oil in a deep-fryer, fry the chicken with the onions until golden, then immerse the chicken (keeping the onions for later) in a large pot of boiling water for 3 minutes. Now transfer to another large pot or casserole, add the remaining soya sauce and rice wine or sherry, salt, Chinese red wine or port and the chicken stock, as well as the onions, and simmer gently for at least 2 hours, turning it over several times during cooking. Serve in a large bowl or in the casserole itself. You will find it very similar in flavour to the French *Coq au vin.*

GREEK

LEMON CHICKEN

*Chicken flavoured with lemon is a delicious combination of
tastes that is commonly found in Greece. There is plenty of sauce
in this dish so rice would be a welcome accompaniment.*

SERVES 6–8

50 g/2 oz butter
1.6 kg/3½ lb prepared chicken,
    without giblets, cut into small
    portions
salt and freshly ground black
    pepper, to taste
300 ml/½ pt boiling water

1 bunch spring onions, trimmed and
    cut into 2.5 cm/1 in pieces
3 eggs
45 ml/3 tbsp freshly squeezed lemon
    juice
2 tbsp chopped fresh dill, to garnish

◆ Melt the butter in a large, heavy-based saucepan and add the
chicken. Cook for about 5 minutes, or until evenly browned,
turning and rearranging during cooking.

◆ Season the chicken with salt and freshly ground black pepper
and add the boiling water and the spring onions. Cover the pan and
simmer for 35–40 minutes, or until the chicken is tender and
cooked through.

◆ Place the eggs in a small bowl and beat well. Gradually whisk in
the lemon juice, a little at a time to prevent curdling. Whisk in
300 ml/½ pt of the cooking liquid from the chicken. Pour the egg
and lemon mixture over the chicken and stir continuously until the
sauce has thickened slightly. Do not boil.

◆ Transfer the chicken and sauce to a warm serving dish and
sprinkle with the chopped fresh dill.

MUSCAT-BAKED ALMOND CHICKEN

This dish is made with the sweet white-green grapes that have been grown around Cyprus and the Levant since Crusader times. Both a wine-making and a dessert grape, the muscat gives a pungent flavour and aroma to this recipe, which has its roots in a centuries-old tradition of using ground almonds as a thickening agent. In Lebanon, the herbs used would be wild – the marjoram, in particular, of a type found only in the eastern Mediterranean.

SERVES 6

2 kg/4½ lb free-range chicken
salt and freshly ground black pepper
½ tsp cinnamon
large pinch of nutmeg
fresh lemon thyme
fresh marjoram
225 g/8 oz muscat grapes, skinned, seeded and halved

250 ml/8 fl oz sweet muscat wine
15 g/½ oz butter
3 tbsp sliced blanched almonds
50 g/2 oz ground almonds
150 ml/¼ pt single cream
2 egg yolks

◆ Preheat the oven to 200°C/400°F/Gas Mark 6. Wash the chicken and pat dry with absorbent kitchen paper. Rub it all over with salt and pepper to taste, the cinnamon and the nutmeg. Take 2–3 sprigs of lemon thyme and the same of marjoram and put them inside the chicken. Place it in a casserole, stuff with half the grapes and pour over the wine. Cover and cook in the oven for 1½ hours.

◆ Remove the chicken from the oven and transfer it to a warm serving dish. Remove the grapes and herbs from the cavity, joint the chicken and cover it with foil to keep it warm.

◆ In a small saucepan, melt the butter and sauté the sliced almonds for a few minutes until just coloured. Remove with a slotted spoon and set aside. Skim the fat from the chicken cooking juices in the casserole and strain them into the saucepan. Heat the juices gently until very hot, but not boiling, and stir in the remaining grapes and the ground almonds. Allow to cook for a few minutes to combine.

◆ In a small bowl, beat the cream and egg yolks together lightly. Take a spoonful of the hot chicken stock and stir it into the egg. Remove the saucepan from the heat and stir in the egg mixture; the sauce should thicken as you stir.

◆ Pour some of the sauce over the jointed chicken and sprinkle it with the toasted almonds. Pour the remainder into a sauceboat to be served with pilau rice.

CHICKEN WITH POUNDED ALMOND SAUCE

SERVES 4

2 garlic cloves, finely chopped
30–60 ml/2–4 tbsp olive oil
1 thick slice bread
1.25 kg/2¾ lb corn-fed chicken, in pieces
salt and freshly ground black pepper
125 ml/4 fl oz chicken stock
10 strands saffron soaked in a little stock

125 ml/4 fl oz *fino* sherry or Montilla
1 bay leaf, crumbled
25 toasted almonds
1 tbsp parsley, chopped almost to a paste
pinch of ground ginger
pinch of ground clove
5 ml/1 tsp lemon juice

◆ Fry the garlic quickly in 30 ml/2 tbsp oil in a wide, shallow casserole. Remove to a blender or mortar. Over a high heat, fry the bread quickly in the oil on both sides then reserve.

◆ Season the chicken pieces and fry them until golden on all sides (a corn-fed chicken should not need more oil). Remove from the pot and drain off any fat. Add the stock, saffron and *fino*, stirring to deglaze the bottom. Return the chicken pieces and add the bay leaf. Cook gently, covered, for 10 minutes.

◆ Grind the toasted almonds in the blender or mortar with the garlic, adding the bread in pieces, parsley and remaining spices. Stir this aromatic purée into the chicken juices with the lemon juice and serve.

HONEY-RUM CHICKEN WITH MUSHROOM SAUCE

SERVES 4

4 large chicken breasts, boned, skinned and fat cut off
50 ml/2 fl oz orange juice
15 ml/1 tbsp honey
20 g/¾ oz clarified butter
2 cloves garlic, crushed
125 g/4 oz button mushrooms, sliced
125 g/4 oz oyster mushrooms, sliced

250 ml/8 fl oz dark rum
450 ml/¾ pt chicken stock
salt and freshly ground black pepper
100 ml/4 fl oz single cream
2 eggs, beaten
2 tbsp chopped fresh coriander
orange slices, to garnish (optional)

◆ Poke several holes in the chicken breasts with a knife point. Mix the orange juice and honey and marinate the chicken in it for 20 minutes. In a large, heavy-based frying pan, brown the chicken in 15 g/½ oz clarified butter. Remove from the heat and set aside.

◆ Melt the remaining butter in the same frying pan, then add the garlic and mushrooms and fry for 1 minute. Pour in the rum and flame it. Add the chicken stock, salt and pepper and chicken and simmer over a low heat for 30 minutes. Just before serving, beat the cream with the eggs and add to the frying pan. Cook over low heat for about 1 minute. Add the coriander, check the seasoning and cook for a further 1 minute. Garnish with orange slices, if desired, and serve.

BRAISED FIVE-SPICE DUCK

SERVES 4–6

2 kg/4½ lb duck
2 slices root ginger, peeled
2 spring onions
60 ml/4 tbsp soya sauce
60 ml/4 tbsp rice wine or sherry
50 g/2 oz icing sugar

1 tsp five-spice powder
1 carrot
750 g/1½ lb Chinese cabbage
6–8 Chinese dried mushrooms,
    soaked

◆ Cut the duck into four pieces (two breasts, two legs and thighs). Place them in a large pot or casserole of boiling water; boil rapidly for 4–5 minutes, then discard two-thirds of the water and add the root ginger, spring onions, soya sauce, rice wine or sherry, icing sugar and five-spice powder. Bring it to a boil again, then put on the lid tightly and simmer gently for 1 hour.

◆ Meanwhile, cut the carrot into small slices, the cabbage into large chunks; add these and the mushrooms to the pot; continue cooking for 30 minutes. Serve with rice.

MINCED DUCK WITH CROÛTONS

SERVES 4–6

125 g/4 oz cooked duck meat
600 ml/1 pt stock
50 g/2 oz peas
10 ml/2 tsp rice wine or dry sherry
1 tsp salt

½ tsp monosodium glutamate
1 tbsp cornflour mixed with 15 ml/
    1 tbsp water
1 tsp chicken fat
3 slices white bread

◆ Finely mince the duck meat. Add it to the stock together with the peas, rice wine or sherry, salt and monosodium glutamate. Bring it to the boil over a high flame, then slowly pour in the cornflour and water mixture. When it boils again, stir in the chicken fat, and remove.

◆ Fry the bread, cut into small cubes, until they become golden and crispy; drain and place them on a soup plate, pour the minced duck all over them so they make a sizzling noise and serve at once before the fried bread croûtons become soggy.

GARLIC ROASTED DUCK

SERVES 4

15 ml/1 tbsp Nuoc Mam sauce or
    light soya sauce
150 ml/¼ pt red wine vinegar
1 onion, chopped
12 juniper berries, crushed
2 tsp fennel seeds

1 clove garlic, crushed
4 duck breast and wing portions
150 g/5 oz tub plain yoghurt
salt and black pepper
watercress, to garnish

◆ Mix the Nuoc Mam sauce, vinegar, onion, juniper berries, fennel seeds and garlic thoroughly in a large bowl and rub well into the duck portions. Cover the bowl with some kitchen film and leave in a refrigerator for 8 hours, turning occasionally.

◆ Preheat the oven to 220°C/425°F/Gas Mark 7. Drain and reserve the marinade. Place the duck portions, skin side down, in an ovenproof dish. Put in the oven for 30 minutes, basting at least once. Turn the duck portions over, baste and cook for a further 30 minutes, basting at least once. Switch off the oven but leave the duck in it.

◆ Spoon 250 ml/8 fl oz of the marinade into a hot pan, cover and allow to simmer for at least 5 minutes. Strain, whisk in the yoghurt and season with salt and black pepper to taste.

◆ Serve the duck on a dish garnished with the watercress. The sauce is served in a bowl. If guests are not proficient with chopsticks, the duck should be chopped into bite-sized pieces.

Above: Garlic Roasted Duck

AROMATIC AND CRISPY DUCK

SERVES 6–8

1.75–2.25 kg/4–5 lb duck
vegetable oil for deep-frying

Cooking Sauce
1.5 litres/2½ pt good stock
   (see p.12)
75 g/3 oz sugar

6 slices fresh root ginger
150 ml/¼ pt soya sauce
60 ml/4 tbsp yellow bean paste
90 ml/6 tbsp rice wine or dry sherry
6 pieces star anise
½ tsp five-spice powder
¼ tsp pepper

◆ Mix the ingredients for the cooking sauce together in a large saucepan. Clean the duck thoroughly and cut in half down the backbone. Place into the liquid and submerge.

◆ Simmer the duck gently for 2 hours. Remove from the cooking liquid and leave to cool. When required, heat the oil in a wok or deep-fryer. When hot, place the duck gently in the oil and fry for 10–11 minutes. Drain well and serve.

DUCK WITH ORANGES AND OLIVES, SEVILLE STYLE

The original "duck with orange" comes from the city that introduced bitter oranges to Europe in the 11th century. Their juice and the olives make the duck seem fatless. Since it is a party dish, an elegant modern presentation is given here.

SERVES 4

1 oven-ready duck (preferably grey barbary)	200 ml/7 fl oz *fino* sherry or Montilla
salt and freshly ground black pepper	1 Seville orange (or 1 sweet orange plus ½ lemon)
30 ml/2 tbsp olive oil	1 bay leaf
1 onion, finely chopped	8–10 parsley stalks, bruised
1 green sweet pepper, seeded and chopped	150–300 ml/5–10 fl oz duck stock from giblets (or chicken stock)
1 large tomato, skinned, seeded and chopped	2 large winter carrots
	150 g/5 oz green olives, rinsed
1 tbsp flour	

◆ Quarter the duck, removing the backbone, visible fat and hanging skin. Season and prick the remaining skin well. Heat the oil in a small casserole and brown the duck on all sides.

◆ Remove the duck and all but 2 tbsp fat from the casserole. Fry the onion in this fat until soft, adding the pepper and tomato halfway through. Sprinkle with flour and stir in. Add the *fino* and stir until simmering.

◆ Fit the duck pieces back into the casserole compactly, tucking in the backbone and 2 strips of thinly pared orange zest. Slice the orange, and lemon, if using (do not peel) and tuck these around the duck, pushing in the bay leaf and parsley stalks. Add enough stock to almost cover and simmer, with the lid on, for 45 minutes.

◆ Quarter the carrots lengthwise, remove the cores and cut them into olive-sized lengths. Round the corners with a knife to make oval shapes. Simmer them in boiling water for 5 minutes.

◆ Remove the duck pieces and discard the backbone, parsley stalks, orange strips and bay leaf. Purée the sauce through a vegetable mill rather than a blender. Return the duck to the casserole and pour in the sauce.

◆ Add the olives and carrot shapes and simmer for another 10 minutes until the carrots are tender.

◆ Move the duck pieces to a serving dish with a slotted spoon. Surround with the carrots and olives and keep warm. If there is too much sauce, boil to reduce it a little. Any floating fat can be removed by pulling strips of absorbent kitchen paper across the surface. Check the seasonings and adjust if necessary, pour the sauce over the duck and serve.

PEKING DUCK

SERVES 6–8

1.5–1.75 kg/3–4 lb duck	100–120 ml/7–8 tbsp yellow bean paste
1 medium cucumber	40 g/1½ oz sugar
1 bunch spring onions	5 ml/1 tsp sesame seed oil
Sauce	Chinese pancakes
30–45 ml/2–3 tbsp vegetable oil	

◆ Wash and dry the duck thoroughly. Hang it up in a well-ventilated place overnight to dry the skin. Cut the cucumber into matchstick-sized shreds. Cut the spring onions into similar-sized shreds.

◆ Place the duck on a wire rack over a roasting dish. Place in a preheated oven at 400°F/200°C/Gas Mark 6 for 1 hour 10 minutes. (It is important to make sure the oven is correctly preheated for a good result.) Do not open the oven door during the roasting – the duck requires no basting.

◆ Meanwhile, to make the sauce, heat the oil in a small saucepan. When hot, add the yellow bean paste and stir over low heat for 2–3 minutes. Add the sugar and 45 ml/3 tbsp water and stir for another 2–3 minutes. Finally, add the sesame seed oil and stir for a further 30 seconds.

◆ Slice the crispy skin off the duck with a sharp knife. Cut into 4 × 5 cm/1½ × 2 in pieces and arrange on a heated plate. Carve the meat into similar-sized pieces and arrange on a separate heated plate. Brush each pancake with 5–7 ml/1–1½ tsp of sauce, and add a little shredded cucumber and spring onion. Place a little duck skin and meat overlapping on each pancake. Roll up, turning up one end of the pancake to stop the filling falling out. Eat using the fingers.

CANTONESE ROAST DUCK

SERVES 4–6

2–2.5 kg/4½–5 lb duck
1 tsp salt

Stuffing
15 ml/1 tbsp vegetable oil
25 g/1 oz sugar
30 ml/2 tbsp rice wine or sherry
15 ml/1 tbsp yellow bean sauce
15 ml/1 tbsp hoisin sauce
½ tsp five-spice powder

2 slices root ginger, peeled and finely
    chopped
2 spring onions, finely chopped

Coating
60 ml/4 tbsp honey
15 ml/1 tbsp vinegar
1 tsp cochineal
350 ml/12 fl oz water

◆ Clean the duck well; pat dry with a cloth or absorbent kitchen paper inside and out. Rub both inside and out with salt, then tie the neck tightly with string so that no liquid will drip out when it is hanging head downward.

◆ To make the stuffing, heat up the oil in a saucepan, mix in the sugar, rice wine or sherry, bean sauce and hoisin sauce, five-spice powder, root ginger and spring onions. Bring to a boil, pour it into the cavity of the duck and sew it up securely.

◆ Plunge the whole duck into a large pot of boiling water for a few seconds only; take it out and baste it thoroughly with the coating mixture then hang it up to dry for at least 4–5 hours, ideally overnight in a well ventilated place.

◆ Preheat the oven to 200°C/400°F/Gas Mark 6. Roast the duck hanging on a meat hook with its head down; place a tray of cold water in the bottom of the oven to catch the drippings. After 25

minutes or so, reduce the heat to 180°C/350°F/Gas Mark 4 and roast for a further 30 minutes, basting once or twice during the cooking with the remaining coating mixture. When it is done let it cool for a while, then remove the strings and pour the liquid stuffing out. Use as the sauce when serving the duck.

PARTRIDGES IN WINE WITH NEW POTATOES

Shooting partridges is a common sport in the hills behind Toledo, where this dish comes from, and they are trapped all over the country as they fly through on their twice-yearly migration. The birds are set off beautifully by the piquant wine sauce.

SERVES 6

3 fat partridges, wishbones removed
salt and freshly ground black pepper
45 ml/3 tbsp olive oil
1 big Spanish onion, chopped
3 garlic cloves, finely chopped
3 bay leaves

1 strip lemon zest
175 ml/6 fl oz dry white wine
60 ml/4 tbsp sherry vinegar
about 200 ml/7 fl oz chicken stock
24 baby new potatoes
chopped fresh parsley

◆ Choose a flameproof casserole into which the birds fit snugly, then salt and pepper them inside and out. Fry the birds in the oil, turning them over and propping them against the sides of the pan, until they are coloured on all sides. Remove and keep warm.

◆ Fry the onion in the same oil, adding the garlic when it softens. Bed the birds down into the onion. Add the bay leaves, lemon zest, wine, vinegar and sufficient stock to cover the legs. Simmer, covered, over a low heat for about 15 minutes.

◆ Meanwhile, simmer the potatoes in boiling salted water for 10 minutes. Move to the casserole, pushing them into the spaces between the birds (add more stock if absolutely necessary) and cook until they are done.

◆ Remove the potatoes and the birds. Halve the partridges and arrange in a warm serving dish, then surround them with the potatoes. Keep warm. Discard the bay leaves and lemon zest and blend the remaining contents of the casserole. Reheat and check the seasonings (if extra stock was needed, boil to reduce a little). Pour a little over the birds and sprinkle with parsley. Pass the remaining sauce round in a jug.

Above: Partridges in Wine with New Potatoes

Fish
AND
Shellfish

*T*ropical waters teem with fish, often as
beautiful as they are flavoursome.
Caribbean cooks know a thing or two about
fish dishes, while Spanish sailors have their
own recipes for cooking aboard ship.
Worldwide, cooks make the most of the
local catch.

CRAB WITH FERMENTED BEANS AND PEPPERS

FISH AND SHELLFISH

SERVES 4–6

2 crabs (approximately 450 g/1 lb each)
2 red chilli peppers
1 green sweet pepper
4 pieces root ginger
3 spring onions
2 cloves garlic
450 ml/¾ pt groundnut oil
3 tsp salted, fermented soya beans

120 ml/4 fl oz stock or chicken soup

Seasoning
1 tsp sugar
1 tsp salt
10 ml/2 tsp oyster sauce
½ tsp monosodium glutamate (optional)
10 ml/2 tsp rice wine or dry sherry

◆ Clean the crabs and chop the flesh of each into 6 pieces. Mince the chilli and the green pepper. Slice the ginger and cut the spring onions into 2 cm/¾ inch pieces. Crush and chop the garlic.

◆ Heat the oil in a pan and add the crab, ginger and spring onions. Fry for 2 minutes and remove from the pan to drain. Reheat the pan to smoking point and add 15 ml/1 tbsp oil. Fry the garlic and beans for 10 seconds, then return the crab to the pan.

◆ Mix the seasoning ingredients with the stock or chicken soup and add the mixture to the pan. Turn and stir the contents for 30 seconds. Serve.

PRAWN TAMARINDO

98

Here's a yummy prawn dish with a quite unusual flavour, thanks to the tamarind it contains. Add a crisp salad and serve on steamed rice.

SERVES 4

25 g/1 oz butter or margarine
2 tbsp minced onion
1 clove garlic, crushed
1 green sweet pepper, cored, seeded and chopped
30 ml/2 tbsp tomato purée
50 ml/2 fl oz sherry
1 bay leaf
120 ml/4 fl oz tamarind juice (see p.9)

30 ml/2 tbsp clear honey
¼ tsp ground allspice
¼ tsp salt
⅛ tsp hot pepper sauce
450 g/1 lb prawns, shelled and deveined
15 ml/1 tbsp fresh lime or lemon juice

◆ Heat the butter in a large frying pan. Add the onion, garlic and green pepper and fry until tender. Add the tomato purée, sherry, bay leaf, tamarind juice, honey, allspice and salt, stirring constantly until heated through. Reduce the heat and simmer, uncovered, until slightly thickened, about 5 minutes. Add hot pepper sauce to taste. Add the prawns and stir until pink, 3–5 minutes. Remove the bay leaf and stir in the lime or lemon juice.

SEAFOOD JAMBALAYA

*Jambalaya is traditionally made with ham, but it's not
a necessity. You may add 125–225 g/4–8 oz chopped ham back in,
if you desire, but bear in mind that you may need to decrease
the seasonings.*

SERVES 6–8

30 ml/2 tbsp vegetable oil
1 onion, chopped
1 green sweet pepper, chopped
2 sticks celery, chopped
3 cloves garlic, finely chopped
3 large tomatoes, seeded and
chopped
250 ml/8 fl oz tomato sauce
250 ml/8 fl oz seafood stock
50 g/2 oz choppd fresh parsley

2 bay leaves
1 tbsp fresh thyme or 1 tsp dried
1 tsp salt
¼ tsp black pepper
½ tsp cayenne pepper
large pinch of white pepper
1 kg/2 lb fresh prawns, crabmeat,
crayfish or oysters, or any
combination, prepared
125 g/4 oz spring onions, chopped

◆ Heat the oil in a deep frying pan. Sauté the onion, green pepper, celery and garlic until they are limp, about 5 minutes. Add the tomatoes, tomato sauce, stock, parsley and seasonings and simmer gently until the tomatoes are cooked down and some of the liquids have reduced. Taste and adjust the seasonings.

◆ Add the seafood. (If using oysters, cut into bite-sized pieces and add in the last 2–3 minutes of cooking.) Simmer just until the prawns are opaque and tightly curled, 5–7 minutes. Just before serving, mix in the spring onions. Serve over rice.

SPANISH

ST JAMES'S BAKED SCALLOPS

Every restaurant in the old town of Santiago offers this dish on St James's Day, for scallops have always been identified with the Saint and scallop shells are still the badge of pilgrims to his shrine. Galician scallops are huge, with creamy orange roes and big white muscles. Tomatoes and brandy make a splendid sauce for them.

SERVES 4

400 g/14 oz shelled scallops (preferably 2–3 big ones on the shell per person)
15 g/½ oz butter
45 ml/3 tbsp oil
60 ml/4 tbsp *aguardiente* (*eau-de-vie*) or brandy
1 onion, finely chopped
3 garlic cloves, finely chopped
200 g/7 oz ripe tomatoes, skinned and seeded (or use canned tomatoes)

1 tsp paprika
pinch of cayenne pepper
120 ml/4 fl oz dry white wine or fish stock
salt and freshly ground black pepper
2–3 tbsp fine breadcrumbs
1 tbsp chopped fresh parsley

◆ In Galicia the scallops are cooked in the curved upper shell. Ask for these at the fishmonger (or use small dishes). To clean fresh scallops, hold a knife flat against the shell and cut the flesh free, then remove the ring of gristle round the white. Pull away any dark gut at the root of the coral.

◆ Heat the butter and 15 ml/1 tbsp oil and quickly fry the scallops for 2 minutes on each side. Shelled or defrosted scallops make a lot of liquid, so remove them when cooked then boil this off.

◆ Warm the spirit in a ladle, flame it and pour over the scallops. Then spoon them into the upper shells or small heatproof dishes.

◆ Add another 30 ml/2 tbsp oil to the pan and fry the onion gently, adding the garlic as it softens. Add the chopped tomatoes, paprika and cayenne pepper and cook until the tomato has reduced to a sauce. Moisten with the wine or fish stock, add salt and pepper to taste and spoon over the scallops.

◆ Mix the breadcrumbs and parsley and sprinkle thinly over the top of the scallops. Heat through for 2–3 minutes under a low grill and serve immediately.

STIR-FRIED PRAWNS IN GARLIC AND TOMATO SAUCE

SERVES 5–6

350 g/12 oz peeled prawns, fresh or
   frozen
1 tsp salt
¾ tsp cornflour
1 egg white
2 cloves garlic
2 spring onions
2 small firm tomatoes
90 ml/6 tbsp vegetable oil

Sauce
30 ml/2 tbsp tomato sauce or purée
¼ tsp salt
15 g/½ oz sugar
pinch of monosodium glutamate
   (optional)
90 ml/6 tbsp good stock (see p.12)
1½ tbsp cornflour blended with
   45 ml/3 tbsp water
5 ml/1 tsp sesame seed oil

◆ Toss the prawns in the salt, dust with the cornflour and coat in the egg white. Crush the garlic. Cut the spring onions into shreds. Skin the tomatoes and cut into eighths.

◆ Heat the oil in a wok or frying pan. When hot, stir-fry the prawns over high heat for 1½ minutes. Remove from the wok or pan. Pour away the excess oil and reheat the wok or pan. When hot, stir-fry the garlic, half the spring onions and the tomatoes over high heat for 30 seconds. Add the tomato purée, salt, sugar, monosodium glutamate, if using, and stock and continue stir-frying for another 30 seconds. Stir in the blended cornflour until the sauce thickens. Sprinkle on the sesame seed oil and remaining spring onions. Return the prawns to the wok or pan, stir once more and serve.

BAHAMIAN GRILLED LOBSTER TAIL

This dish is ideal for a summer barbecue.

SERVES 4

4 lobster tails (about 750 g/1½ lb in
   total), thawed if frozen, removed
   from shells intact and deveined
20 ml/4 tsp fresh lime or lemon juice
4 cloves garlic, minced
75 g/3 oz ghee or unsalted butter
125 g/4 oz dry breadcrumbs
2 tsp salt
1 tsp freshly ground black pepper
½ tsp dried thyme, crumbled

½ tsp dried marjoram, crumbled
½ tsp dried oregano, crumbled
½ tsp dried basil, crumbled
½ tsp dried rosemary, crumbled
½ tsp dried sage, crumbled
½ tsp garlic powder
¼ tsp minced hot pepper or hot
   pepper sauce
2 tbsp freshly grated Parmesan
vegetable oil

◆ Rinse the lobster shells and dry with absorbent kitchen paper, then sprinkle them with lime or lemon juice. In a small saucepan, cook the garlic in ghee or butter over moderate heat for about 1 minute. Remove the pan from the heat.

◆ In a shallow bowl, stir together the breadcrumbs, salt, pepper, thyme, marjoram, oregano, basil, rosemary, sage, garlic powder, hot pepper or hot pepper sauce and Parmesan cheese. Roll the pieces of lobster meat in the garlic butter, dredge them in the breadcrumb mixture and return them to their shells.

◆ Brush the barbecue grill with oil. Prepare the barbecue according to the manufacturer's directions. Grill the tails, shell sides down, on a rack set 10–15 cm/4–6 in over the coals, for 10 minutes, turning them occasionally from side to side. Cover the grill and grill the tails for 5–10 minutes more or until they are just cooked through.

CANTONESE GINGER AND ONION CRAB OR LOBSTER

FISH AND SHELLFISH

102

EXOTIC CUISINES

SERVES 5–6

1.5 kg/3 lb crab or 1 kg/2 lb lobster
5 slices fresh root ginger
4 spring onions
1 medium red sweet pepper
vegetable oil for deep-frying

½ tsp salt
150 ml/¼ pt good stock (see p.12)
30 ml/2 tbsp light soya sauce
45 ml/3 tbsp rice wine or dry sherry
5 ml/1 tsp sesame seed oil

◆ Scrub the crab thoroughly under running water. Chop the crab into 4 pieces, discarding the grey "dead men's fingers". Alternatively, scrub the lobster under running cold water and chop into bite-sized pieces, discarding the hard stomach sac behind the head and the black intestinal vein. Crack the claws with the back of a chopper. Cut the ginger and spring onions into matchstick-sized shreds. Thinly slice the red pepper.

◆ Heat the oil in a wok or deep-fryer. When very hot, add the crab or lobster pieces one by one to the oil. Fry over high heat for 2½ minutes. Remove and drain. Pour away the oil to use for other purposes, reserving about 30 ml/2 tbsp. Reheat the wok or frying pan. When hot, stir-fry the ginger, spring onion, red pepper and salt over medium heat for 1 minute. Pour in the stock, soya sauce and rice wine or sherry. Bring to the boil and return the crab or lobster to the wok or pan. Toss a few times, then cover and cook for 3–4 minutes until the sauce is reduced by half. Sprinkle on the sesame seed oil, toss and transfer to a heated serving dish.

MUSSEL PANCAKES

Galician mussels are the best in the world and this simple recipe shows them off perfectly. The thin crêpes are related to the ones made in Brittany, which shares the same Celtic culture. Sweet ones are made with milk and filled with custard for dessert. Savoury crêpes may also be made with blood at pig-killing time.

SERVES 4

1.75 kg/4 lb mussels	**For the Crêpes**
120 ml/4 fl oz dry white wine	100 g/3½ oz flour
2 tbsp chopped onion	2 large eggs
4 parsley stalks, bruised	45–60 ml/4–6 tbsp double cream
6 black peppercorns, crushed	about 50 g/2 oz butter
	6 tbsp chopped fresh parsley

◆ Wash the mussels, discarding any that are open and do not close when touched. Pull off the beards. Put the wine, onion, parsley stalks and peppercorns in a big pan and bring to a simmer. Put in the mussels (in 2 batches) and cover tightly. Cook over a high heat for 3–4 minutes shaking occasionally, until they are open. Discard the shells and any that remain shut or smell strongly. Strain the liquid into a measuring jug and leave to cool. Taste for seasoning.

◆ Make the crêpe batter. Put the flour in a bowl or blender and work in the eggs, mussel liquor and 30 ml/2 tbsp cream. (Don't overbeat in a blender.) Let it stand, if you can, for an hour.

◆ Melt 20 g/¾ oz butter in a frying pan, swirling it round. Add to the batter and stir thoroughly. Heat another 7 g/¼ oz butter and swirl. Use about ⅓ of a cup of batter per crêpe: it is easier to pour from a cup. Lift the pan and pour the batter fast into the middle of the pan and in a circle around, tilting the pan to cover the base. (If you overdo the liquid, spoon off anything that doesn't set at once: crêpes should be thin.)

◆ Put the pan back over the heat, shaking it to make sure the crêpe does not stick. Cook for a minute until golden underneath, then flip over with a fish slice (picking up with fingers is just as easy). Briefly fry the other side. Roll and keep warm on a plate while you make more crêpes.

◆ Warm the remaining cream in a saucepan with the mussel bodies. Spoon mussels and a little cream onto one edge of a crêpe, sprinkle with chopped parsley and roll up. Serve the crêpes as quickly as possible.

PRAWN CREOLE

SERVES 4–6

30 ml/2 tbsp vegetable oil	1.5 litres/2½ pt chicken stock
1 large onion, chopped	750 g/1½ lb prawns, shelled and
8 cloves garlic, minced	deveined
2 large sticks celery, finely chopped	225 g/8 oz can sliced water
4 medium tomatoes, chopped	chestnuts, drained and rinsed or
2 medium green sweet peppers,	225 g/8 oz jicama, sliced
chopped	7 ml/½ tbsp lime juice
30 ml/2 tbsp tomato purée	salt and freshly ground black pepper
5 ml/1 tsp hot pepper sauce	750 g/1½ lb cooked white
½ tsp dried oregano	long-grain rice
1 tsp dried thyme	1 tbsp minced coriander or parsley
10 ml/2 tsp Worcestershire sauce	to garnish

◆ Heat the oil in a large saucepan, frying pan or wok. Add the onion, garlic, celery, tomatoes and peppers and fry over moderate heat until tender. Then add the tomato purée, hot pepper sauce, oregano and thyme and blend, stirring constantly, for about 2 minutes. Add the Worcestershire sauce and chicken stock and bring to the boil over medium-high heat until thickened, about 30 minutes. Add the prawns and water chestnuts and simmer, uncovered, until the prawns are opaque throughout, about 4 minutes. Remove from the heat and adjust the seasoning with more hot pepper sauce to taste, lime juice and salt and pepper. Serve over or under a scoop of rice on warm dishes and sprinkle the top with coriander or parsley. Serve immediately.

STEAMED LOBSTER

SERVES 2–4

1 lobster, weighing about
    750 g–1 kg/1½–2 lb

Sauce
15 ml/1 tbsp oil
2 spring onions, finely chopped
2 slices root ginger, finely chopped

1 tsp salt
1 tsp sugar
60 ml/4 tbsp good stock (see p.12)
freshly ground Sichuan pepper
½ tbsp cornflour
5 ml/1 tsp sesame seed oil

◆ Steam the lobster for 20 minutes. Leave to cool, then split in 2 lengthwise, and cut each half into 4 pieces.

◆ Crack the shell of the lobster claws so that the flesh can be taken out easily.

◆ Make the sauce by heating up the oil in a wok or saucepan; toss in the onions and root ginger; add salt, sugar, stock and ground pepper. Thicken with the cornflour mixed with a little water. Finally add the sesame seed oil; pour it all over the lobster and serve immediately.

CRAB-STUFFED FISH

Use whole trout, red snapper, red mullet, plaice or sole for this dish, cooked individually if you use small fish. Alternatively, present an elegant platter of a large, stuffed fish surrounded by lemon slices and parsley sprigs. Fresh crabmeat is best but frozen or canned are acceptable.

SERVES 4

25 g/1 oz butter
6 spring onions, chopped
125 g/4 oz coarsely chopped
    mushrooms
1 tbsp chopped fresh parsley
1 clove garlic, finely chopped
¼ tsp salt
¼ tsp paprika
¼ tsp black pepper

2 tbsp grated Parmesan cheese
50 ml/2 fl oz double or single cream
225 g/8 oz fresh crabmeat,
    picked over
4 whole fish, about 225 g/8 oz each,
    cleaned and boned
salt and freshly ground black pepper
flour for dredging (optional)
olive oil or melted butter

◆ Preheat the oven to 180°C/350°F/Gas Mark 4.

◆ Melt the butter in a small frying pan. Sauté the onions, mushrooms, parsley and garlic until limp, about 5 minutes. Stir in the salt, paprika, pepper, Parmesan and cream until well mixed. Add the crab, stirring gently. Set aside.

◆ Rinse the fish and pat dry with absorbent kitchen paper. Season the insides lightly with salt and pepper. You may dredge it in flour at this point if you wish, covering the outside only with a thin coat of flour, and shaking off excess.

◆ Stuff the fish with the crab mixture, then skewer it closed with toothpicks, or sew a few large stitches with coarse thread. Put the fish in a lightly oiled baking tin and brush with olive oil or drizzle with melted butter.

◆ Bake the fish until the flesh at the thickest point is opaque but still juicy, about 10 minutes. Do not wait for the fish to flake easily, because it continues cooking after it is removed from the oven and would be overcooked by the time you serve it.

> NOTE: If you use one large fish, a 1.25–1.5 kg/2½–3 lb fish
> will serve 4–5 people.

POTATOES WITH CUTTLEFISH, CLAMS AND PEPPERS

This is a simple dish of potatoes in a green sauce with sea flavours that come from two sorts of shellfish. A cuttlefish looks like a plump money purse with a frill around it and is best for stewing. They can be replaced by squid but buy one big one as little ones are too tender for anything but frying.

SERVES 4

2 cuttlefish (about 450 g/1 lb together)
60 ml/4 tbsp olive oil
2 garlic cloves
1 onion, chopped
50 g/2 oz raw ham or smoked bacon, diced
450 g/1 lb clams or mussels, cleaned, or 150 g/5 oz shelled cockles

2 green sweet peppers, seeded and cut into strips
1 kg/2 lb potatoes, peeled and diced
salt and freshly ground black pepper
6 tbsp chopped fresh parsley
5 saffron strands
50 ml/2 fl oz white wine

◆ Prepare the cuttlefish. Grip the tentacles and use them to pull out the insides. Cut across above the eyes and discard everything below. Large cuttlefish and squid have a mouthpiece in the centre of the tentacles which can be popped out like a button.

◆ Slit the body up both sides and remove the cuttle bone. Squid have a spinal structure like transparent plastic, which will pop out when the body is flexed. Rub off the skin with salt-coated fingers and wash. Cut off the squid's fins and cut the body into thick, wide rings. Rinse inside and cut into thick strips. Separate the tentacles.

◆ Put 30 ml/2 tbsp oil in a casserole and fry the garlic cloves until they colour. Remove at once to a mortar. Add another 30 ml/2 tbsp oil and fry the onion and ham over a medium heat. When the onion starts to colour, add the shellfish and cook. Add the peppers and stir for 2 minutes. Pack in the potatoes and pour in 600 ml/1 pt of water to barely cover. Season with salt and bring to a simmer.

◆ In a mortar, mash the garlic to a paste, working in 2 tbsp parsley, the saffron and wine. Stir, with some pepper, into the casserole. Cook until the potatoes are almost tender (about 20 minutes). Take off the lid halfway through to evaporate some of the liquid.

◆ Add the cuttlefish or squid and simmer for 2 more minutes. Check the seasonings and sprinkle with the remaining parsley.

SARDINES COOKED WITH TOMATOES AND ROSEMARY

It has been said that once you have tasted this classic Greek dish, you'll dream of Greece forever.

SERVES 8

8 fresh sardines, cleaned, heads
   removed
flour, for coating
olive oil, for shallow frying

Sauce
50 ml/2 fl oz olive oil
1 tbsp plain flour
50 ml/2 fl oz red wine vinegar
400 g/14 oz can chopped tomatoes

2 tsp dried rosemary, or 3 tsp
   chopped fresh rosemary
1 tsp dried oregano
2 garlic cloves, crushed
salt and freshly ground black
   pepper, to taste
1 tsp sugar
fresh rosemary sprigs, to garnish
lemon wedges, to serve

◆ Wash the sardines and pat dry with absorbent kitchen paper. Lay out on a chopping board and dredge with flour on both sides.

◆ Heat the oil and cook the fish, in batches, for about 5 minutes, or until golden and cooked through. Using a slotted spoon, transfer the fish to a dish lined with absorbent kitchen paper to drain. Tent the fish with kitchen foil to keep warm.

◆ To make the sauce, heat the olive oil in a medium-sized saucepan and stir in the flour to make a paste. Cook for 30 seconds, then gradually stir in the red wine vinegar and add the chopped tomatoes, rosemary, oregano and garlic. Season with salt and freshly ground black pepper and stir in the sugar. Cover and simmer for 15–20 minutes, until thickened, stirring occasionally.

◆ Arrange the sardines on a warm serving platter and pour the sauce over them. Garnish with fresh rosemary sprigs and serve with lemon wedges.

MIXED FISH AND SHELLFISH STEW

SERVES 6 OR MORE

1.25 kg/2¾ lb fish, cleaned
75 ml/5 tbsp olive oil
750 g/1½ lb onions, chopped
450 g/1 lb clams, mussels etc, cleaned
salt and freshly ground black pepper
1½ tbsp paprika

10 black peppercorns, crushed
1 *guindilla* or ½ dried chilli, seeded and chopped
freshly grated nutmeg
8–10 tbsp chopped parsley
350 g/12 oz shrimps or small prawns
475 ml/16 fl oz dry white wine

◆ Cut off spines and fins from the fish with scissors and remove all scales by stroking the fish from the tail to the head with the back of a knife or your thumbs. Rinse the fish inside and cut off heads (freeze to use for stock). Cut whole fish across into sections about 5 cm/2 in long and fillets into similar-sized pieces.

◆ Warm 30 ml/2 tbsp oil in the bottom of your chosen pot. Put in a good bed of onions. On this arrange a layer of one-third of the fish, choosing from the different varieties. Pack half the clams or mussels into all the spaces. Season with salt, ½ tbsp of paprika, half the peppercorns, a little ground pepper and *guindilla* or chilli and the nutmeg. Sprinkle with 15 ml/1 tbsp oil and plenty of parsley. Make a bed of shrimps or prawns on top.

◆ Repeat all the layers. Make a top layer of fish, seasoning as before and packing onion into the gaps. Add more parsley. Add the wine and about 200 ml/7 fl oz of water to almost cover the fish. Then re-season the top layer, adding ½ tbsp of paprika and another 15 ml/1 tbsp of oil.

◆ Bring to simmering (the best part of 10 minutes), then cover, turn down the heat and simmer for 15 minutes. Check the broth seasoning and lay spoons as well as knives and forks on the table so that everyone can taste it.

BRAISED MUSSELS WITH BEAN CURD AND MUSHROOMS

SERVES 5–6

1.5 litres/2½ pt mussels
4 slices root ginger
6 medium dried Chinese mushrooms
2 cakes fresh bean curd
3 cloves garlic
3 spring onions
450 ml/¾ pt good stock (see p.12)
60–75 ml/4–5 tbsp rice wine or dry sherry

½ tsp salt
pepper to taste
1 chicken stock cube
1 tbsp cornflour blended with 30 ml/ 2 tbsp water
5 ml/1 tsp sesame seed oil

◆ Scrub the mussels thoroughly. Poach in a large saucepan of simmering water with the ginger for 1½ minutes, then drain. Discard any unopened ones. Transfer the mussels to a large pan or flameproof casserole. Soak the dried mushrooms in hot water to cover for 25 minutes. Drain and discard the tough stalks. Cut the mushroom caps into quarters. Cut the bean curd into cubes or rectangles. Finely chop the garlic. Shred the spring onions.

◆ Place the pan of mussels over medium-high heat. Pour in the stock and wine or sherry, then add the bean curd, mushrooms, garlic, half the spring onion, salt and pepper. Bring to the boil and sprinkle in the crumbled stock cube. Stir, then simmer gently for 10 minutes. Stir in the blended cornflour. Sprinkle with the remaining spring onion and the sesame seed oil.

CAJUN

ALMOND TROUT

*The classic method for preparing this dish is to coat the trout
with flour or breadcrumbs, then pan-fry them. Here the trout is
grilled with just a little olive oil and paprika, then a crunchy
topping of almonds and spring onions is added. The result is a
simpler dish with a wonderful flavour that saves a few calories.*

SERVES 2

2 small trout, about 450 g/1 lb each,
    filleted with the heads removed
    (can be whole or in 2 pieces)
30 ml/2 tbsp olive oil
½ tsp paprika
40 g/1½ oz butter
75 g/3 oz sliced blanched almonds

5 ml/1 tsp Worcestershire sauce
10 ml/2 tsp lemon juice
1 tsp grated lemon zest
few drops of Tabasco sauce
3 spring onions, chopped
2 tbsp chopped fresh parsley

◆ Oil the grill rack. Put the trout on the rack, skin side down.
Combine the olive oil and paprika and brush over the trout. Put
under the hot grill, about 13 cm/5 in from the heat, and grill
unskinned side up until opaque but still juicy, 5–6 minutes, using a
rule of 10 minutes per 2.5 cm/1 in of the fillet's thickness.
◆ While the fish is cooking, melt the butter in a small frying pan.
Add the almonds and cook until they are a golden brown. Add the
Worcestershire sauce, lemon juice, lemon zest and Tabasco sauce
and mix well. Remove from the heat, add the spring onions and
parsley, and quickly spoon over the grilled trout.

108

ITALIAN

BAKED SEA BASS WITH MAYONNAISE

SERVES 6

1 sea bass (about 1.25 kg/3½ lb)
2 large onions
60 ml/4 tbsp olive oil
2 cloves garlic
2 sprigs rosemary
2 tbsp finely chopped fresh parsley

2 tbsp finely chopped fresh basil
juice of 1 lemon
60 ml/4 tbsp dry white wine
salt and freshly ground black pepper
600 ml/1 pt mayonnaise

◆ Preheat the oven to 180°C/350°F/Gas Mark 4. Clean and descale
the fish.
◆ Very finely slice the onion and make a fish-shaped bed of it on a
large piece of foil. Pour the olive oil over it and lay the fish on top.

◆ Crush the garlic and smear along the inside of the fish, together
with the sprigs of rosemary. Chop the parsley and basil finely, mix
with the lemon juice, and similarly anoint the inside of the fish.
◆ Raise the edges of the foil, pour over the white wine and season.
Seal the parcel carefully, making sure there are no holes or tears.
◆ Set the parcel in an amply-sized dish and bake for 30 minutes.
When ready, remove from the oven, but do not unseal until the
parcel is completely cool.
◆ About 45 minutes before eating, remove the fish from its
wrapper and collect all the juices into a small saucepan. Boil them
down and cool; then add them to the mayonnaise.
◆ Decorate the fish with the onions on which it lay and serve.

Above: Almond Trout

BAKED FISH STUFFED WITH MUSHROOMS

SERVES 4

30 ml/2 tbsp oil

1 onion, sliced and separated into rings

15 g/½ oz root ginger, finely grated

1 tsp chopped mint leaves, fresh or bottled

225 g/8 oz tomatoes, peeled and chopped

½ tsp chilli powder

salt

225 g/8 oz mushrooms, peeled and sliced

450–750 g/1–1½ lb whole fish, such as cod, cleaned

30 ml/2 tbsp lemon juice

◆ Heat the oil in a pan. Add the onion, ginger and mint and fry until the onion is golden.

◆ Add the tomato, chilli powder and ½ tsp salt and cook, mashing the tomato into a thick paste with the back of a wooden spoon.

◆ Add the mushrooms and continue to cook for 6–7 minutes.

◆ Use this mixture to stuff the fish. Lay it in a greased ovenproof dish, sprinkle with the remaining oil and the lemon juice, cover with foil and bake at 175°C/350°F/Gas Mark 4 for 30–35 minutes, until tender.

◆ Remove the skin and serve.

BAKED TROUT WITH POMEGRANATE

SERVES 4

1 large ripe pomegranate
15 ml/1 tbsp olive oil
1 onion, finely chopped
2 garlic cloves, peeled and finely
    chopped
150 g/5 oz coarsely chopped pecans
4 tbsp chopped fresh parsley
salt and freshly ground black pepper

¼ tsp ground cardamom
30 ml/2 tbsp wine vinegar
50 g/2 oz butter or margarine,
    melted
4 trout, 300–350 g/10–12 oz each,
    cleaned
curly kale to garnish

◆ With a sharp knife, cut the top off the pomegranate. Score the fruit in about 6 wedges and pull apart into separate sections. Gently scoop the seeds into a small bowl. Set aside.

◆ In a medium frying pan, over medium-high heat, heat the olive oil. Add the onion and cook until softened and beginning to colour, 3–5 minutes. Add the garlic and cook 1 minute longer.

◆ Stir in the pecans, parsley, salt and pepper to taste, cardamom, vinegar and half the melted butter or margarine. Remove from the heat. Stir in three-quarters of the pomegranate seeds.

◆ Preheat the oven to 200°C/400°F/Gas Mark 6. Lightly grease a large, shallow baking dish. Rinse the fish under cold running water and pat dry with absorbent kitchen paper. Score each fish in two places on each side. Spoon one-quarter of the onion mixture into each fish.

◆ Arrange the fish in a baking dish, drizzle with the remaining butter or margarine and bake, uncovered, until the flesh flakes easily if tested with the tip of a knife, 12–15 minutes. Serve the fish on a bed of curly kale and sprinkle with the remaining pomegranate seeds.

Above: Salmon Trout Stuffed with Black Olives

ITALIAN

SALMON TROUT STUFFED WITH BLACK OLIVES

SERVES 6

1 large salmon trout (about 2 kg/4½ lb)	6 anchovy fillets
225 g/8 oz fresh or canned plum tomatoes, roughly chopped	25 g/1 oz black olives
	60 ml/4 tbsp dry white wine
60 ml/4 tbsp olive oil	30 ml/2 tbsp white wine vinegar
4 cloves garlic	30 ml/2 tbsp brandy
2 sprigs fresh rosemary	salt and freshly ground black pepper

◆ Preheat the oven to 180°C/350°F/Gas Mark 4. Clean and descale the fish.

◆ Spread out the tomatoes on a large sheet of foil. Mix the olive oil with the tomatoes and lay the fish on top.

◆ Crush the garlic and smear the inside of the fish with it; lay the sprigs of rosemary and the anchovy fillets at equal intervals in the cavity. Chop the olives finely and sprinkle half inside, half outside.

◆ Combine the wine, vinegar and brandy and pour over the fish, then lift the sides of the foil and seal the fish carefully. Bake the fish for 35 minutes.

◆ Lift the fish from the foil with a long fish slice when it is cooked. Take care when transferring it so that it does not break, and set it on a serving dish.

◆ Pour all the juices from the foil into a pan and bring them to the boil. Season with the salt and pepper, pour over the fish and serve.

CARIBBEAN

CARIBBEAN RED SNAPPER

Here's a Caribbean treatment of this delectable fish. You'll be surprised how the mélange of spices and tomatoes permeates the fish with West Indian flavours.

SERVES 4

vegetable oil	5 ml/1 tsp hot pepper sauce
1 medium onion, sliced	450 g/1 lb red snapper fillets
1 large tomato, peeled and chopped	7 ml/½ tbsp lime or lemon juice
½ tsp ground allspice	1 small clove garlic, minced
¼ tsp dried oregano	½ large onion, chopped
¼ tsp dried thyme	¼ red sweet pepper, chopped
1 tsp chopped fresh coriander, or to taste	¼ green sweet pepper, chopped
	7 ml/½ tbsp olive oil
½ bay leaf	25 g/1 oz sliced almonds
30 ml/2 tbsp water	

◆ Preheat the oven to 200°C/400°F/Gas Mark 6. Coat a 33 × 23 × 5 cm/13 × 9 × 2 in baking dish with vegetable oil. Arrange the sliced onion in the dish and add the tomato, allspice, oregano, thyme, coriander and bay leaf. Combine the water and hot pepper sauce and gently pour over the tomato mixture. Rub the fish fillets with lime or lemon juice and arrange in the dish.

◆ Fry the garlic, onion and red and green peppers in olive oil for about 3 minutes. Spoon over the fish. Cover and bake in the oven for 40–45 minutes or until the fish flakes easily when tested with a fork. Remove the bay leaf and garnish with the almonds.

INDIAN

FRIED SPICED FISH

SERVES 2

1 onion, finely chopped	1 tsp chilli powder
15 g/½ oz fresh ginger, finely grated	60 ml/4 tbsp oil
6 curry leaves	450 g/1 lb white fish, boned, skinned and cubed
salt	
¼ tsp turmeric	

◆ Pound, grind or blend in a liquidizer the onion, ginger, curry leaves, ½ tsp salt, the turmeric and chilli powder to make a paste.

◆ Spread the paste over the fish and leave to marinate for about 2 hours.

◆ Heat the oil in a large pan that the fish will fit into in one layer, add the fish and fry for about 10 minutes, until tender. Add extra salt to taste and serve.

CHINESE

STEAMED WHOLE FISH WRAPPED IN LOTUS LEAVES

SERVES 4–6

1 whole fish, about 1 kg/2 lb
22 ml/1½ tbsp dark soya sauce
2 lotus leaves
45 ml/3 tbsp vegetable oil

Garnish and sauce
75–125 g/3–4 oz canned snow
    pickles

3 slices root ginger
2 spring onions
2 fresh chillies
30 ml/2 tbsp light soya sauce
30 ml/2 tbsp rice wine or dry sherry
90 ml/6 tbsp good stock (see p.12)
2 tsp sugar

◆ Clean the fish and dry well. Rub inside and out with the soya sauce. Shred the pickles, ginger, spring onions and fresh chillies, discarding the seeds. Soak the lotus leaves in warm water for 10 minutes to soften. Drain.

◆ Heat the oil in a wok or frying pan. When hot, stir-fry the pickles, spring onions, ginger and chillies over medium heat for 1 minute. Add the soya sauce, rice wine or sherry, stock and sugar, bring to the boil and stir for 30 seconds.

◆ Place the fish on the lotus leaves. Pour half the contents of the wok or pan over the length of the fish. Turn the fish over and pour over the remainder. Wrap the fish completely in the lotus leaves. Secure with string. Place in a steamer and steam for 25 minutes.

SPANISH

TROUT IN RED WINE

Trout crowd all the mountain rivers in Spain. This recipe comes from Navarre, though there are two views as to what is the true Navarre way of cooking them. Some say they should be stuffed or garnished with fried ham or bacon – a method that is popular all over Spain. Others say they must be cooked with mountain herbs and the fruity red local wine, as in this recipe.

SERVES 4

2 small trout, cleaned	200 ml/7 fl oz Navarra red or
1 small onion, chopped	another fruity wine
6 black peppercorns, crushed	30–45 ml/2–3 tbsp olive oil
1 bay leaf, crumbled	salt
2 sprigs of thyme	½ tbsp butter
1 sprig of rosemary	½ tbsp flour
4 parsley stalks, bruised	3 tbsp chopped parsley
2 sprigs of mint, plus extra to garnish	new potatoes to serve

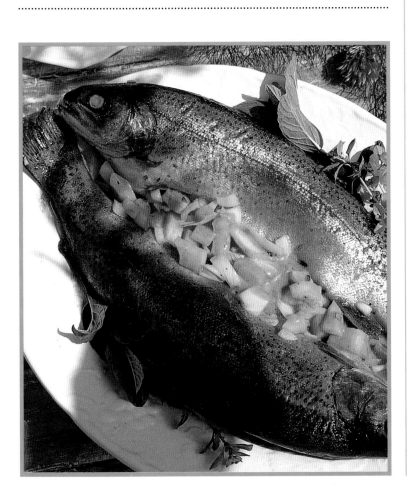

◆ Rinse the cleaned trout, dry them and pack them into a baking dish. Sprinkle with the onion, black peppercorns, crumbled bay leaf, thyme, rosemary, parsley and mint. Pour in the red wine and leave to marinate for 2 hours or so.

◆ Sprinkle the fish with the oil and a little salt and put the dish in the oven, at 190°C/375°F/Gas Mark 5. Cook for 15 minutes for 275 g/9 oz trout, 20 minutes if they are any larger.

◆ Drain off the cooking liquid into a saucepan. Mash together the butter and flour and drop it into the wine mixture to thicken it a little, stirring. Bring back to a simmer, then pour over the trout and sprinkle with parsley. Serve with new potatoes garnished with mint.

VIETNAMESE

CARP COOKED IN COCONUT MILK

This recipe works well with any firm fish steak. Try it with cod, halibut or trout.

SERVES 4

15 ml/1 tbsp vegetable oil	30 ml/2 tbsp Nuoc Mam sauce or
1 stalk lemon grass, peeled and	30 ml/2 tbsp light soya sauce
finely chopped	120 ml/4 fl oz coconut milk (see p.8)
½ tsp peppercorns, bruised	1 carp, large enough to serve 4,
1 clove garlic, chopped and crushed	cleaned and gutted
1 red chilli pepper, thinly sliced	rind and juice of 1 lime
½ tbsp ground cinnamon	1 tbsp fresh coriander, finely
4 whole cloves, bruised	chopped

◆ In the oil, gently fry the lemon grass, peppercorns, garlic, chilli, cinnamon and cloves until the flavours are released – 2 minutes at the outside.

◆ Add the Nuoc Mam sauce and stir in gently. Remove from the heat and stir in the coconut milk.

◆ Place the carp in a pan and pour over the coconut milk mixture. Add the lime juice and fresh coriander and stir. Cover and simmer for 10–15 minutes or until the fish is cooked.

◆ Remove the fish and place on a serving dish. Garnish with the strips of lime rind. Heat the sauce and boil for a few minutes to reduce and thicken. Strain until a plain milk is left. Pour this over the carp.

GREEK

SMALL FISH IN VINE LEAVES

Vine leaves are perfect for wrapping around small, oily fish to hold in the flavours and to prevent the fish from falling apart during cooking. This is an attractive and unusual Greek speciality which works successfully on the barbecue.

SERVES 6

6 small mackerel or herring, scaled and cleaned	3 tsp dried thyme or 4 tsp fresh thyme
juice of 1 lemon	12 vine leaves, boiled for 5 minutes, drained and rinsed
salt and freshly ground black pepper	fresh thyme sprigs, to garnish
olive oil, to drizzle	lemon wedges, to serve

◆ Wash the fish under cold running water and pat dry with absorbent kitchen paper. Place on a chopping board and sprinkle with lemon juice. Season with salt and freshly ground black pepper. Drizzle evenly with olive oil and sprinkle with thyme.

◆ Lay the vine leaves out on the work surface and lightly brush with a little olive oil. Use two of the vine leaves to wrap around each fish, completely encasing it.

◆ Arrange the fish on a lightly oiled grill rack and cook under a preheated grill for about 6 minutes on each side, or until it flakes easily and is cooked through. Transfer to a serving platter and garnish with fresh thyme sprigs. Serve with lemon wedges.

SPANISH

FISH STEW WITH RED PEPPERS AND POTATOES

SERVES 4–5

60 ml/1 tbsp olive oil	3 canned pimentoes
1 onion, chopped	150 ml/¼ pt dry white wine
550 g/1¼ lb bonito tuna belly or 2–3 small mackerel, filleted	1 dried chilli, seeded and chopped
2 garlic cloves, finely chopped	450 g/1 lb potatoes, cubed
salt and freshly ground black pepper	2 tsp paprika
400 g/14 oz canned tomatoes with juice	2 tbsp chopped fresh parsley

◆ Heat the oil in a shallow casserole big enough to take the fish. Fry the chopped onion gently, adding the garlic when it softens.

◆ Cut the fish into serving pieces and season well. Push the onion to the sides of the casserole and fry the fish on both sides.

◆ Add the tomatoes and pimentoes, breaking them up with a spoon, and the wine and chilli. Distribute the potatoes over the top, sprinkling with paprika and more salt and pepper. Add enough water to cover everything well. Cook for about 20 minutes or until the potatoes are done and the liquid has reduced somewhat. Check the seasonings, add parsley and serve in soup bowls.

BRAISED WHOLE FISH IN HOT VINEGAR SAUCE

SERVES 4–6

2 slices root ginger
1 whole fish, about 750 g–1 kg/
   1½–2 lb
1 tsp salt
pepper to taste
60 ml/4 tbsp vegetable oil

Sauce
3 slices root ginger
40 g/1½ oz canned bamboo shoots,
   drained

½ red sweet pepper
1 small carrot
1 green chilli
2 dried chillies
2 spring onions
25 g/1 oz lard
30 ml/2 tbsp light soya sauce
45 ml/3 tbsp good stock (see p.12)
90 ml/6 tbsp vinegar
½ tbsp cornflour blended with
   30 ml/2 tbsp water

◆ Finely chop the 2 slices of ginger. Clean the fish and dry well. Rub evenly inside and out with salt, pepper, chopped ginger and 15 ml/1 tbsp of the oil. Leave to season for 30 minutes.

◆ Shred the 3 slices of ginger, bamboo shoots, red pepper, carrot, chillies, discarding the seeds, and spring onions.
◆ Heat the remaining oil in a wok or frying pan. When hot, fry the fish for 2½ minutes on each side. Remove and drain. Add the shredded ginger, bamboo shoots, red pepper, carrot, chillies and spring onions to the remaining oil and stir-fry over medium heat for 1 minute. Add the lard, soya sauce, stock and half the vinegar and cook for another minute.
◆ Lay the fish back in the wok or pan and cook gently for 2 minutes on both sides, basting. Transfer the fish to a serving dish. Stir the remaining vinegar into the wok, then add the blended cornflour, stirring over high heat until the sauce thickens.
◆ Pour the sauce from the wok over the length of the fish and garnish with the shredded vegetables.

FISH AND SHELLFISH

117

EXOTIC CUISINES

NUEVO CUBANO

RED SNAPPER WITH CITRUS

If red snapper is not available, substitute any white, firm-fleshed fish. This is a recipe that leans toward classic, but the citrus takes it out of the ordinary.

SERVES 4

15 ml/1 tbsp olive oil

2 shallots, minced, or white part of 4 spring onions, trimmed and thinly sliced

225 g/8 oz fresh mushrooms, trimmed and thinly sliced

120 ml/4 fl oz freshly squeezed orange juice

120 ml/4 fl oz bottled clam juice

½ tsp salt

freshly ground black pepper

red snapper, perch, turbot or sole fillets, about 125 g/4 oz each

3 heaped tbsp minced fresh parsley

◆ In a large frying pan over medium heat, heat the oil. Add the shallots and cook for about 1 minute. Add the mushrooms and cook for 1 more minute to soften slightly. Add the juices and bring to a boil. Cover and simmer gently until the mushrooms are completely tender, 5–7 minutes. Uncover and boil over high heat until the liquid is somewhat thickened, about 5 minutes. Season with half the salt and pepper to taste.

◆ Place the fish fillets over the mushrooms. Sprinkle with the remaining salt and pepper to taste. Reduce the heat to medium low, cover and steam the fillets until they are just opaque in the centre and flake easily when tested with the tip of a knife, 6–8 minutes. (Alternatively, bake, covered, at 180°C/350°F/Gas Mark 4 for 15 minutes.) Sprinkle the fish with parsley and serve immediately.

JEWISH

RED SNAPPER WITH GREEN SAUCE

SERVES 6

vegetable oil for greasing
1.5–1.75 kg/3–4 lb red snapper or
    sea bass fillets
juice of 5 limes
salt and freshly ground black pepper

Sauce
1 head romaine lettuce, trimmed,
    cored and shredded
½ cucumber, peeled and seeded
1 small green sweet pepper, cored,
    seeded and chopped

1 red onion, quartered
3–4 garlic cloves
1 small bunch watercress, stems
    trimmed
4–5 spring onions, trimmed
3 tbsp coriander leaves

To garnish
cherry tomatoes
ripe olives
chopped fresh coriander leaves

◆ Lightly grease a deep baking dish. Place the fish in the centre of the dish and rub with a little lime juice. Sprinkle with salt and pepper to taste. Set aside.

◆ Make the sauce. In a food processor fitted with metal blade, process the lettuce, cucumber, green pepper, red onion, garlic, watercress, spring onions and coriander leaves with the remaining lime juice. Pour the sauce over the fish, cover and refrigerate for at least 2 hours.

◆ Preheat the oven to 180°C/350°F/Gas Mark 4. Uncover the fish and bake, basting twice, until the fish is opaque and the flesh flakes when pierced with a knife, 20–25 minutes. Remove the fish to a serving dish. Pour the sauce over and garnish with cherry tomatoes, ripe olives and coriander leaves.

SPANISH

BISCAY BAY SOLE WITH CREAM AND SHELLFISH

The superb fish we know as Dover sole in the English Channel is fished all across the Bay of Biscay, right down to the Basque coast. This type of rich old-fashioned cooking, with a cream sauce, has been typical for a century or more. Shellfish make the perfect garnish and done this way they provide the stock for the dish.

SERVES 4

2 tbsp chopped onion
6 black peppercorns
4 tbsp chopped fresh parsley
1 bay leaf
200 ml/7 fl oz dry white wine
16 medium-size clams or mussels,
    cleaned

50 g/2 oz butter
4 Dover sole (or plaice) fillets
about 1½ tbsp flour
120 ml/4 fl oz whipping cream
salt and ground white pepper
    (optional)

◆ Put the chopped onion in a saucepan with the peppercorns, 2 tbsp parsley, the bay leaf and the wine. Bring to a simmer. Put in the clams or mussels, cover and cook for 1–2 minutes until they open. Remove the shellfish then let the liquid boil for 5 minutes and reserve. Take one shell off each mussel (discarding any that are still shut).

◆ Melt the butter in a frying pan. Dust the fish fillets in seasoned flour and fry (probably two at a time) for a couple of minutes on each side. Remove to a warm serving plate and keep warm.

◆ Add 1 tsp flour to the pan and stir into the butter. Strain in the reserved shellfish stock, add the cream and stir to deglaze the pan. Boil to reduce the sauce by half, adding the shellfish, face upwards, to warm them. This sauce should need no seasoning, but taste to check. Pour over the sole, sprinkle with parsley and serve. Slim leeks make good partners for this dish.

Above: Calypso Cod Steaks

CALYPSO COD STEAKS

These cod steaks have zip, thanks to the hot peppers. Salmon works well, too, but do not use salted cod.

SERVES 6

45 ml/3 tbsp lime juice
30 ml/2 tbsp olive oil
2 tsp minced garlic
1 tsp minced hot pepper or 10 ml/
 2 tsp hot pepper sauce

6 cod or salmon steaks, 2 cm/¾ in
 thick and weighing about 175 g/
 6 oz each

◆ In a bowl, whisk together the lime juice, olive oil, garlic and hot pepper or hot pepper sauce.
◆ Brush the grill rack with oil and preheat the grill. Grill the steaks for about 10–12 minutes on one side, basting frequently with the sauce, then turn and cook on the other side for another 10–12 minutes, again basting frequently, until done but not overcooked.

MACKEREL SIMMERED IN SAKE

SERVES 4

4 mackerel fillets, about 75 g/3 oz
 each
pinch of salt
200 ml/7 fl oz sake

100 ml/3½ fl oz mirin
50 ml/2 fl oz dark soya sauce
2 tbsp shredded root ginger, to
 garnish

◆ Rinse the fillets in cold water and pat dry. Arrange the fillets on a strainer and sprinkle with a little salt; set aside to drain for at least 1 hour. Rinse in cold water and pat dry.
◆ With a sharp knife, cut each fillet into 3 or 4 pieces. In a large saucepan, bring the sake to a simmer. Arrange the fish in a single layer in the simmering sake, dark side uppermost, and bring the sake rapidly back to the boil. This process blanches the mackerel.
◆ Add the remaining ingredients except the ginger, bring to the boil and carefully skim the surface. Cover and cook over high heat for about 10 minutes until the flesh is tender and the stock is reduced by two-thirds.
◆ Turn off the heat and leave the fish in the hot stock for a few minutes. Carefully remove the fish from the stock with a fish slice and arrange the fillets in individual bowls. Garnish with the ginger and spoon the stock over the fish.

NUEVO CUBANO

NUTTY ROASTED RED SNAPPER

*Deservedly one of the most sought-after fishes for a sumptuous
meal, snapper warrants a gorgeous presentation.*

SERVES 4

15 ml/1 tbsp olive oil
6 red snapper fillets, 1 cm/½ in thick
30 ml/2 tbsp ghee (clarified butter)
1 tsp chopped fresh thyme leaves
⅛ tsp freshly ground black pepper

⅛ tsp salt
50 g/2 oz plus 1 tbsp toasted
   pumpkin seeds or almond slivers
   for garnish (optional)

◆ Preheat the oven to 240°C/475°F/Gas Mark 9. Grease a baking tray with 15 ml/1 tbsp olive oil and place the fillets in it. Brush the fillets with 30 ml/2 tbsp ghee, then sprinkle with thyme, pepper and salt. Bake for 4 minutes. Sprinkle with toasted pumpkin seeds or almond slivers and serve.

JEWISH

JEWISH-STYLE FRIED FISH

*Introduced by Sephardic Jews in the 1600s, fried fish is now a
favourite Friday night supper among many Jewish communities.
Somehow it tastes better cold than hot, so it is an ideal choice for
a Sabbath supper, as it can be prepared early in the day. Be sure to
fry in oil, not butter, and keep in a cool place, not the refrigerator
if possible, as the fish will stay crisper much longer. A mixture of
half medium and half fine matzo meal is best for the coating.*

SERVES 6

1.5 kg/3 lb fish fillets or steaks, such
   as flounder, halibut, salmon,
   herring, or any combination
salt
75 g/3 oz plain flour
2 eggs, beaten
¼ tsp freshly ground black pepper

175 g/6 oz matzo meal
vegetable oil for frying

To garnish
lemon wedges
parsley sprigs

◆ Rinse the fish fillets or steaks in cold water and sprinkle lightly with salt. Place in a colander and leave to drain for 30 minutes. Pat dry with absorbent kitchen paper.

◆ Place the flour, beaten eggs, seasoned with black pepper, and matzo meal in three pie dishes or shallow dishes. Dip each piece of fish first into the flour, shaking off any excess, then into the egg, brushing to coat evenly, and finally into the matzo meal. Be sure the fish is completely coated with meal to prevent any moisture escaping during frying.

◆ In a deep-fat fryer or large frying pan, over medium-high heat, heat about 1 cm/½ in vegetable oil to 180°C/350°F. Add several pieces of fish and fry until the underside is well browned, 4–5 minutes. Gently turn the fish and fry until the other side is brown, 3–4 minutes. Drain on absorbent kitchen paper.

◆ Continue frying in batches until all the fish is fried, adding more oil as necessary. (Do not try to fry too many pieces at a time or the temperature of the oil will fall too low and the fish will stew rather than fry.)

◆ Arrange the fish on a serving dish and store in a cool place, loosely covered. Serve with lemon wedges and parsley sprigs. (The fish can be served hot; keep it warm in a 180°C/350°F/Gas Mark 4 oven until all the fish is cooked, then serve at once.)

Above: Nutty Roasted Red Snapper

CARIBBEAN

POACHED SALMON FILLETS WITH DILL-AND-GINGER VINAIGRETTE

This recipe uses a cold water fish but gives it a Caribbean spice treatment. Serve with a rice-and-beans dish.

SERVES 4

4 × 175 g/6 oz boneless salmon
   fillets with skin on
9 large sprigs of fresh dill
1 bay leaf
4 whole cloves
salt
9 whole black peppercorns
30 ml/2 tbsp white wine vinegar

Dill-and-Ginger Vinaigrette
30 ml/2 tbsp French mustard
1 tbsp grated root ginger
2 tbsp finely chopped shallot
1 tsp finely chopped garlic
30 ml/2 tbsp tarragon vinegar
50 g/2 oz canned pimentoes, diced
salt and freshly ground black pepper
120 ml/4 fl oz olive oil

◆ Prepare the vinaigrette by whisking the mustard, ginger, shallot, garlic, vinegar, pimentoes and salt and pepper together in a bowl. Then add the olive oil in a slow stream, whisking rapidly until well blended. Set aside.

◆ Place the salmon fillets in a shallow saucepan with enough water to cover. Add all but one dill sprig, the bay leaf, cloves, salt, peppercorns and vinegar. Bring the water to the boil and simmer for 3–5 minutes. Do not overcook. Drain and serve with the vinaigrette, giving the vinaigrette a last-second whisking, if necessary. Float the reserved sprig of dill on top of the bowl of vinaigrette for decoration.

ITALIAN

BRAISED SWORDFISH WITH PEPPERS

SERVES 4

4 swordfish steaks (about 175 g/6 oz each)
60 ml/4 tbsp olive oil
4 cloves garlic
1 medium onion, roughly chopped
1 medium red sweet pepper

125 g/4 oz fresh or canned plum tomatoes, roughly chopped
1 chilli pepper
150 ml/¼ pt dry white wine
salt and freshly ground black pepper

◆ Wash and thoroughly dry the steaks. Heat the oil over a high heat and seal each steak on each side.

◆ Remove the fish from the pan and set aside. Turn down the heat to medium and add the whole cloves of garlic and the onions.

◆ Turn the heat to high once more and cook the onions until the edges begin to catch. Reduce the flame to a gentle simmer and cook on until the onions and garlic are softened. In the meantime, de-seed and finely slice the peppers.

◆ When the onions are soft, add the peppers and cook until they begin to soften – about 5 minutes. Add the tomatoes, the whole chilli and the wine. Bring to a fierce boil, then add the fish. Turn the heat to a low simmer and cover the pan. Simmer until the fish is very tender, about 15 minutes.

◆ Remove the fish from the pan and set it aside in a warm place. Boil up the pan juices very briskly, until they are reduced to a thick, creamy mixture. Season, pour around the fish and serve.

Above: Barbecued Shark

C A J U N

BARBECUED SHARK

*This barbecue recipe is an easy and tasty way to cook shark, or
other dense-fleshed fish such as swordfish.*

SERVES 4

45 ml/3 tbsp lemon juice
45 ml/3 tbsp lime juice
½ tsp grated lemon zest
½ tsp grated lime zest
50 ml/2 fl oz olive oil
3 tbsp chopped fresh dill

3 cloves garlic, finely chopped
pinch of salt
4 shark steaks, about 175 g/6 oz
    each
freshly ground black pepper

◆ In a glass or other non-reactive dish, combine all the ingredients except the shark and pepper. Place the shark steaks in the marinade, turning to coat thoroughly, and spreading dill and garlic bits over the tops of the fish. Sprinkle with black pepper, cover with clingfilm and refrigerate for about 2 hours, turning once or twice.

◆ When the barbecue coals have stopped flaming, place the shark steaks on a lightly greased grill. Cook for about 5 minutes each side, turning once. (Total cooking time should be about 10 minutes per inch of thickness.) Baste with the extra marinade, if desired. The fish is cooked when the flesh turns opaque but is still juicy.

C H I N E S E

SQUIRREL FISH

*This dish derives its name from the fact that, when cooked and
served, the fish's tail curves up like a squirrel's.*

SERVES 4–6

1 whole fish, about 750 g–1 kg/
    1½–2 lb
3 slices root ginger
1½ tsp salt
pepper to taste
20–25 g/¾–1 oz cornflour
vegetable oil for deep-frying

Sauce
2 tbsp wood ears (tree fungus)

6 medium dried Chinese mushrooms
2 spring onions
25 g/1 oz canned bamboo shoots,
    drained
25 g/1 oz lard
45 ml/3 tbsp soya sauce
15 g/½ oz sugar
60 ml/4 tbsp good stock (see p.12)
30 ml/2 tbsp wine vinegar
30 ml/2 tbsp rice wine or dry sherry

◆ Clean the fish and slit open from head to tail on the underside so that it lies flat. Cut 7–8 deep slashes on one side of the fish and only 2 on the other side.

◆ Finely chop the ginger. Rub the fish inside and out with the salt, pepper and ginger, then coat in the cornflour. Soak the wood ears and mushrooms separately in hot water to cover for 25 minutes. Drain and discard the tough stalks. Cut the mushroom caps into shreds. Finely slice the wood ears. Cut the spring onions into 5 cm/2 in sections. Slice the bamboo shoots.

◆ Heat the oil in a wok or deep-fryer. When hot, gently fry the fish over medium heat for 4 minutes, then reduce the heat to low. Meanwhile, melt the lard in a smaller wok or pan. When hot, stir-fry the wood ears, mushrooms, spring onions and bamboo shoots over medium heat for 1½ minutes. Add the soya sauce, sugar, stock, vinegar and wine or sherry. Stir the ingredients over low heat for about 2 minutes.

◆ Raise the heat under the wok containing the fish and fry for another 2 minutes. The tail should have curled by now due to the uneven amount of cuts on the fish. Lift out the fish, drain and place on a heated dish to serve.

Vegetables, Pulses
AND
Rice

Vegetables, pulses and rice are important staples in many parts of the world. Rice and peas is a thrifty way of obtaining perfect protein and one which will appeal to the growing number of vegetarians; aubergines, beans, tomatoes and mangetouts combine to make delicious vegetable pots.

CAULIFLOWER BAKED WITH TOMATOES AND FETA

This dish is enlivened with a strong flavour of tomatoes combined with the typically Greek use of ground cinnamon to give that extra special taste.

SERVES 4–6

85 ml/3 fl oz olive oil
1 onion, sliced
2 garlic cloves, crushed
8 tomatoes, seeded and chopped
large pinch of ground cinnamon
2 tsp dried oregano

salt and freshly ground black
    pepper, to taste
1 large cauliflower, cut into florets
15 ml/1 tbsp freshly squeezed lemon
    juice
75 g/3 oz feta cheese, grated

◆ Heat 30–45 ml/2–3 tbsp olive oil in a heavy-based frying pan and sauté the onion and garlic for about 3–4 minutes, or until the onion has softened.

◆ Add the chopped tomatoes, cinnamon and oregano and season with salt and pepper. Stir and simmer, covered, for 5 minutes.

◆ Preheat the oven to 190°C/375°F/Gas Mark 5. Add the cauliflower to the tomato mixture, cover, and simmer for a further 10–15 minutes or until the cauliflower is just tender. Remove from the heat.

◆ Transfer the cauliflower and tomato mixture to a large, shallow dish and drizzle over the remaining olive oil. Sprinkle over the lemon juice and grated feta. Bake for 45–50 minutes, or until the cauliflower is soft and the cheese has melted. Serve warm.

130

HOT AND SOUR CUCUMBER SICHUAN STYLE

SERVES 4–6

1 cucumber
1 tsp salt
25 g/1 oz sugar

30 ml/2 tbsp vinegar
15 ml/1 tbsp chilli oil

◆ Split the cucumber in two lengthwise and then cut each piece into strips rather like potato chips. Sprinkle with the salt and leave for about 10 minutes to extract the bitter juices.

◆ Drain the cucumber strips. Place on a firm surface and soften by gently tapping with the blade of a cleaver or knife.

◆ Place the cucumber strips on a plate. Sprinkle the sugar evenly over them and then add the vinegar and chilli oil just before serving the dish.

ARMENIAN VEGETABLE STEW

There are no hard and fast rules to making this very Armenian speciality. It can contain meat to make it more substantial – tender pieces of lamb sautéed before adding the vegetables – while the latter are an amalgam of whatever is in the garden, for example, substitute turnip for carrots, cabbage for celery.

SERVES 4–6

75 ml/3 fl oz olive oil
4 cloves garlic, crushed
225 ml/8 fl oz beef stock or
   consommé
1 bay leaf
½ tsp dried tarragon
½ tsp dried oregano
salt and freshly ground black pepper
2 medium carrots, halved and thinly
   sliced
125 g/4 oz fresh stringless green
   beans, cut into 1 cm/½ in lengths
2 small potatoes, peeled and diced

2 sticks celery, halved lengthwise
   and thinly sliced
1 courgette, thinly sliced into rounds
1 small aubergine, halved and thinly
   sliced
1 small red onion, thinly sliced
1 small cauliflower, broken into
   florets
½ red sweet pepper, cored, seeded
   and cut into strips
½ green sweet pepper, cored,
   seeded and cut into strips
75 g/3 oz shelled fresh peas

◆ Preheat the oven to 180°C/350°F/Gas Mark 4. Place the oil in a large enamelled or stainless steel casserole and warm it over medium heat. Add the garlic and stir to flavour the oil, about 2 minutes. Pour in the beef stock or consommé and add the bay leaf, herbs and seasoning to taste. Bring to the boil.

◆ Add the vegetables, little by little, stirring to combine as you add them. Cover the casserole with a lid or foil and transfer to the oven. Bake for about 1 hour or until the vegetables are all tender, stirring occasionally. Serve as a vegetarian main course or as a side dish.

CHICKPEAS WITH SPINACH

*A Friday Lent dish in many Spanish households, this soup-stew is
made with or without salt cod. The latter makes a pleasant
vegetarian dish.*

SERVES 6

200 g/7 oz salt cod, soaked overnight (optional)	2 garlic cloves, finely chopped
300 g/10 oz chickpeas, soaked overnight	2 ripe tomatoes, skinned and chopped
2 onions, 1 whole, peeled, chopped	1 tsp paprika
1 clove	salt and freshly ground black pepper
1 big carrot	850 g/1¾ lb spinach, trimmed and washed
1 bay leaf	2 hard-boiled eggs, peeled and chopped
2–3 parsley stalks, bruised	
45 ml/3 tbsp olive oil	

◆ Remove the bones and skin from the salt cod (if using) and shred the flesh. Put the drained chickpeas, salt cod, 1 whole onion stuck with a clove, whole carrot, bay leaf and parsley stalks into a big casserole and add 1.2 litres/2 pt water. Bring slowly to a simmer, skim off the bubbles then cover and simmer for 1½–2 hours.

◆ Heat the oil in a frying pan and fry the chopped onion. As it softens add the garlic, tomatoes and paprika. Cook down to a sauce, seasoning with salt and pepper.

◆ Add the spinach to a saucepanful of boiling water – just in and out for young spinach, but cook older leaves for 2–3 minutes. Drain and chop.

◆ When the chickpeas are almost tender, remove the bay leaf, parsley stalks, whole onion and carrot. Discard the clove and purée the onion and carrot in a blender or food processor with 3 tbsp chickpeas and half a ladleful of their liquid. Check the overall amount of liquid: the chickpeas should barely be covered at this point. Pour off some water if necessary.

◆ Add the tomato sauce and onion purée to the casserole. Taste for seasoning – plenty is needed. Add the spinach, simmer for another 20 minutes or so to blend the flavours, then check that the chickpeas are tender. This dish is traditionally served with chopped hard-boiled egg on top.

SHANGHAI EMERALD FRIED RICE

SERVES 4–6

225 g/8 oz spring greens or cabbage	450 g/1 lb cooked rice
2 tsp salt	2 tbsp chopped ham
75 ml/5 tbsp vegetable oil	¼ tsp monosodium glutamate (optional)
2 eggs	
2 spring onions	

◆ Wash and finely shred the spring greens or cabbage. Sprinkle with 1½ tsp of the salt. Toss and leave to season for 10 minutes. Squeeze dry. Heat 22 ml/1½ tbsp oil in a wok or pan. When hot, stir-fry the cabbage for 30 seconds. Remove from the pan.

◆ Add 15 ml/1 tbsp oil to the wok or pan. When hot, add the beaten eggs to form a thin pancake. As soon as the egg sets, remove from the pan and chop. Chop the spring onions.

◆ Heat the remaining oil in a wok or pan. When hot, stir-fry the spring onion for a few seconds. Add the rice and stir with the spring onion. Reduce the heat to low, stir and turn until the rice is heated through. Add the cabbage, two-thirds of the egg and the ham. Stir and mix them together well. Sprinkle with monosodium glutamate, if using, and the remaining salt. Stir and turn once more, then sprinkle with the remaining egg.

Above: Garbanzo Beans with Spinach

BEAN CURD WITH MUSHROOMS

SERVES 4–6

3–4 medium dried Chinese mushrooms	½ tsp sugar
	15 ml/1 tbsp sherry
4 cakes fresh bean curd	5 ml/1 tsp sesame seed oil
60 ml/4 tbsp oil	1 tsp cornflour
½ tsp salt	15 ml/1 tbsp soya sauce

◆ Soak the dried mushrooms in warm water for about 30 minutes. Squeeze them dry and discard the stalks. Keep the water for use as stock. Slice each square of bean curd into 6 mm/¼ in slices and then cut each slice into 6 or 8 pieces.

◆ Heat the oil in a wok and stir-fry the mushrooms for a short time. Add about 150 ml/¼ pt of the water in which the mushrooms have been soaking. Bring to the boil and add the bean curd with the salt and sugar. Let it bubble for a while and then add the sherry and the sesame seed oil. Mix the cornflour with the soya sauce and a little water in a bowl and pour it over the bean curd in the wok so that it forms a clear, light glaze. Serve immediately.

HOPPIN' JOHN

134

This dish is undoubtedly African in origin. No one quite knows how it got its name, but each Caribbean cook seems to have his or her own recipe for this mixture of rice and black-eyed peas. Folklore holds that eating it on New Year's Day brings good luck, probably because the dish is so filling you won't want for much more. Unfortunately, it also brings fat and cholesterol when cooked in the traditional manner with knuckle of bacon or pig cheeks. This recipe is a healthier version. If you wish to make a vegetarian meal, just skip the meat altogether.

SERVES 4

700 ml/1¼ pt water	275 g/10 oz long-grain white rice
2 chicken stock cubes	450 g/1 lb can black-eyed peas,
1 medium ripe tomato, chopped	drained and rinsed
10 spring onions, chopped	175 g/6 oz cooked ham, trimmed of
1 bay leaf	fat and cut in bite-sized cubes
1 tsp dried thyme	salt and freshly ground black pepper
5 ml/1 tsp hot pepper sauce	

◆ Bring the water, stock, tomato, spring onions, bay leaf, thyme and hot pepper sauce to the boil in a large saucepan. Add the rice, cover, and simmer until tender, about 25 minutes. Stir in the black-eyed peas and ham, season, cover, and simmer for 8–10 minutes.

JEWISH

LATKES

Latkes are a well-known and well-loved vegetable dish in the Jewish repertoire. Cooked in oil, these potato pancakes are traditional at Hanukah because they symbolize the miracle of the oil which lasted eight days. They are delicious with rich roast poultry, such as duck and goose, but can also be eaten as a brunch dish or on their own sprinkled with sugar or topped with apple sauce or sour cream.

SERVES 6–8

6 medium potatoes, peeled	1 tsp salt
1 onion	pinch of ground white pepper
2 eggs, lightly beaten	vegetable oil for frying
50 g/2 oz fine matzo meal or plain flour	apple sauce or sour cream for serving

◆ In a food processor fitted with a grater attachment, grate the potatoes and onion. Drain in a colander, pressing to squeeze out as much liquid as possible. Place in a large bowl and beat in the remaining ingredients except the oil and accompaniments. (Work as quickly as possible so the potatoes do not turn brown.)

◆ In a large heavy frying pan, over medium-high heat, heat about 1 cm/1 in vegetable oil or just enough to cover the pancakes. Drop the batter by tablespoonsful into the hot oil and cook until the underside is browned, 2 minutes. Turn and cook until the second side is browned, 1–2 minutes longer.

◆ Remove to a serving dish and keep warm in a 180°C/300°F/Gas Mark 4 oven. Continue until all the batter has been used, adding a little more oil if necessary. Serve the latkes immediately with apple sauce or sour cream.

LAYERED AUBERGINE, POTATO AND TOMATO CASSEROLE

SERVES 6

2 medium aubergines
salt and freshly ground black pepper
9 small potatoes, peeled and sliced
2 large Spanish onions, chopped
90 ml/6 tbsp olive oil
2 garlic cloves, finely chopped
2 large green sweet peppers,
    seeded and sliced

1 large red sweet pepper, seeded
    and sliced
9–10 tbsp chopped parsley
3 × 400 g/14 oz cans tomatoes
2 tsp paprika
45 ml/3 tbsp red wine vinegar

◆ Slice the aubergine very thinly, lay the slices out on the draining board and sprinkle with salt. Leave to sweat for 30–40 minutes, then blot with absorbent kitchen paper. Cook the potatoes for 15 minutes in boiling salted water. Soften the onions in 60 ml/4 tbsp oil over a low heat, then add the garlic.

◆ Grease an earthenware dish or casserole (about 30 cm/12 in across and at least 7.5 cm/3 in deep) with oil. Make three layers of vegetables, starting with a third of the potato slices, then the aubergine slices, then the peppers, cooked onion and garlic together with some of the pan oil, plus parsley. Add 1 can tomatoes and their juice, squeezing the tomatoes through clenched fingers to break them up well. Season with salt, pepper and paprika and repeat until all the ingredients are in. Sprinkle vinegar over the second layer and 15 ml/1 tbsp oil over the top of the dish.

◆ Cover with foil and bake in a preheated oven at 200°C/400°F/Gas Mark 6 for 1 hour. Then remove the foil, turn down the heat to 160°C/325°F/Gas Mark 3 and give it another 30–60 minutes to brown and concentrate the juices. Excellent hot or cold, this dish also reheats well.

BAKED AUBERGINES WITH MOZZARELLA

SERVES 4

2 medium aubergines
60 ml/4 tbsp olive oil
450 g/1 lb fresh or canned plum
    tomatoes
2 tbsp fresh oregano or 1 tbsp dried

salt and freshly ground black pepper
225 g/8 oz Mozzarella cheese
3 tbsp freshly grated Parmesan
    cheese

◆ Preheat the oven to 200°C/400°F/Gas Mark 6. Cut off the coarse stalks of the aubergines and slice them lengthwise in 1 cm/½ in slices. Bake the slices in the oven, directly on the wire shelving, for 10 minutes or until very soft.

◆ In the meantime, oil a baking dish. Chop the tomatoes roughly and combine with the oregano. Season strongly with the salt and pepper. Grate the Mozzarella and mix it with the Parmesan.

◆ Remove the aubergine slices from the oven and line the baking dish with one layer. Spread the tomato and oregano mixture evenly over it, and sprinkle the Mozzarella and Parmesan on top of that. Continue these layers until the dish is full, leaving yourself a good amount of Mozzarella and Parmesan as a final thick coating: the cheese will melt and seal the dish as it cooks.

◆ Bake until the cheese melts and browns, about 15–20 minutes.

VEGETARIAN SPRING ROLLS

MAKES 20

1 pack of 20 frozen spring roll skins
225 g/8 oz fresh beansprouts
225 g/8 oz young tender leeks or
   spring onions
125 g/4 oz carrots

125 g/4 oz white mushrooms
oil for deep-frying
1½ tsp salt
1 tsp sugar
15 ml/1 tbsp light soya sauce

◆ Take the spring roll skins out of the packet and leave them to defrost thoroughly under a damp cloth. Wash and rinse the beansprouts in a bowl of cold water and discard the husks and other bits and pieces that float to the surface. Drain. Cut the leeks or spring onions, carrots and mushrooms into thin shreds.

◆ To cook the filling, heat 45–60 ml/3–4 tbsp oil in a preheated wok or frying pan and stir-fry all the vegetables for a few seconds. Add the salt, sugar and soya sauce and continue stirring for about 1–1½ minutes. Remove and leave to cool a little.

◆ To cook the spring rolls, heat about 1.5 litres/2½ pt oil in a wok or deep-fryer until it smokes. Reduce the heat or even turn it off for a few minutes to cool the oil a little before adding the spring rolls. Deep-fry 6–8 at a time for 3–4 minutes or until golden and crispy. Increase the heat to high again before frying each batch. As each batch is cooked, remove and drain it on absorbent kitchen paper. Serve hot with a dip sauce such as soya sauce, vinegar, chilli sauce or mustard.

◆ These spring rolls are ideal for a buffet-style meal or served as cocktail snacks.

SPANISH

MIXED SPRING VEGETABLE POT

A dish which celebrates the new vegetables of spring – using a handful of this, a handful of that! Short lengths of leek, quartered baby fennel bulbs and the trimmed bases of artichokes (or whole baby ones) – whatever is available goes in.

SERVES 3–4

1 onion, chopped
30 ml/2 tbsp olive oil
3 garlic cloves, finely chopped
125 g/4 oz streaky *tocino* or diced ham or bacon with some fat
275 g/9 oz podded peas or broad beans (or frozen beans)
275 g/9 oz green beans, in short lengths

4 small carrots, thickly sliced
50 g/2 oz mangetouts
120 ml/4 fl oz dry white wine
300 ml/½ pt chicken stock
1 hard-boiled egg, peeled, with yolk and white separate
6 tbsp chopped parsley
salt and freshly ground black pepper

◆ Soften the onion in hot oil in a casserole, adding the garlic when the onion is soft. Put in a blender or food processor and set aside.

◆ Fry the ham or bacon in the casserole in their own fat. Add the peas or broad beans, green beans and carrots, laying the mangetouts on top. Add the wine and stock, cover and cook until tender for about 10 minutes.

◆ Purée the onion, garlic, egg yolk and 2 tbsp parsley in the blender or food processor with a little of the cooking liquid. Stir this mixture back into the casserole and season well. Sprinkle with the remaining parsley and chopped egg white.

RED PEPPERS STUFFED WITH VEGETABLES

175 g/6 oz potatoes
50–75 g/2–3 oz butter or ghee
1 small onion, finely chopped
15 g/½ oz fresh ginger, finely grated
1 clove garlic, finely chopped
125 g/4 oz tomatoes, peeled and
　　chopped
½ tsp turmeric

½ tsp chilli powder
salt
½ tsp ground coriander
½ tsp garam masala
leaves from 1 sprig of coriander
4 large red peppers
30 ml/2 tbsp oil

◆ Peel the potatoes, dice them and leave in a pan of cold water to prevent discoloration.

◆ Heat the butter or ghee in a pan, add the onion, ginger and garlic and fry until the onion is golden.

◆ Add the tomato, turmeric, chilli powder, ½ tsp salt and ground coriander and stir briskly, squashing the tomato under the back of a wooden spoon to make a thick paste.

◆ Drain the potato and add to the spice mix with 30–60 ml/ 2–4 tbsp water. Cover and cook on a low heat, stirring occasionally, for 10–15 minutes, until the potato is tender but not soft.

◆ Add the garam masala and coriander leaves. Cook for a further 3–4 minutes, then set aside, covered.

◆ Wash the peppers and, with a sharp knife, cut off the tops, which can be used as lids. Scrape them out and discard the seeds and pith.

◆ Stuff the peppers with the potato curry and replace the lids.

◆ Heat the oil in a pan, put in the peppers and fry gently on all sides until cooked, about 15 minutes. Alternatively, stand the peppers in a greased dish, cover and cook in the oven at 200°C/400°F/Gas 6 for 30 minutes until tender.

AUBERGINE WITH SICHUAN "FISH SAUCE"

4–5 dried red chillies
450 g/1 lb aubergines
oil for deep-frying
3–4 spring onions, finely chopped
1 slice root ginger, peeled and finely
　　chopped
1 clove garlic, finely chopped

1 tsp sugar
15 ml/1 tbsp soya sauce
15 ml/1 tbsp vinegar
15 ml/1 tbsp chilli bean paste
2 tsp cornflour, mixed with 30 ml/
　　2 tbsp water
5 ml/1 tsp sesame seed oil

◆ Soak the dried red chillies for 5–10 minutes, cut them into small pieces and discard the stalks. Peel the aubergines, discard the stalks and cut them into diamond-shaped chunks.

◆ Heat the oil in a wok and deep-fry the aubergines for 3½–4 minutes or until soft. Remove with a slotted spoon and drain.

◆ Pour off the oil and return the aubergines to the wok with the chillies, spring onions, root ginger and garlic. Stir a few times and add the sugar, soya sauce, vinegar and chilli bean paste. Stir for 1 minute. Add the cornflour and water mixture, blend well and garnish with sesame seed oil. Serve hot or cold.

ITALIAN

TAGLIATELLE WITH CHICKPEAS AND BASIL

Pasta and chickpeas with aromatic fresh basil are a wonderful combination.

SERVES 4

60 ml/4 tbsp olive oil
1 clove garlic, crushed
6 tbsp snipped chives
4 sage leaves, chopped
salt and freshly ground black pepper

2 × 400 g/14 oz cans chickpeas, drained
450 g/1 lb tagliatelle verdi
6 basil sprigs

◆ Heat the olive oil, garlic, chives, sage, salt and freshly ground black pepper with the chickpeas in a large saucepan for about 3 minutes. The idea is to heat the ingredients rather than to cook them. Add the drained pasta and toss well. Leave the pan over the lowest heat setting while you use scissors to shred the basil sprigs over the pasta, discarding any tough stalk ends. Mix lightly into the pasta and serve.

SAN SHIAN – "THE THREE DELICACIES"

SERVES 4–6

275 g/9 oz winter bamboo shoots
125 g/4 oz oyster or straw
　mushrooms
60 ml/4 tbsp oil
300 g/10 oz fried gluten or
　deep-fried bean curd

1 ½ tsp salt
1 tsp sugar
15 ml/1 tbsp light soya sauce
5 ml/1 tsp sesame seed oil
fresh coriander leaves to garnish
　(optional)

◆ Cut the bamboo shoots into thin slices. The oyster mushrooms can be left whole if small; otherwise halve or quarter them. Straw mushrooms can be left whole.

◆ Heat the oil in a hot wok or frying pan, swirling it so that most of the surface is well greased. When the oil starts to smoke, add the bamboo shoots and mushrooms and stir-fry for about 1 minute. Add the gluten or bean curd together with salt, sugar and soy sauce. Continue stirring for 1–1 ½ minutes longer, adding a little water if necessary. Finally add the sesame seed oil, blend well and serve hot.

◆ This dish can also be served cold. In that case, you might like to separate the three main ingredients, arrange them in three neat rows and garnish with fresh coriander.

BEGGARS' NOODLES

SERVES 6

3 spring onions
45 ml/3 tbsp soya sauce
45 ml/3 tbsp wine vinegar
450 g/1 lb wheat flour noodles, flat
　or Ho Fen noodles, or spaghetti

Sauce
45 ml/3 tbsp peanut butter
30 ml/2 tbsp sesame paste
45 ml/3 tbsp sesame seed oil

◆ Coarsely chop or shred the onions. Mix the soya sauce and vinegar together. Mix the peanut butter, sesame paste and sesame seed oil together.

◆ Place the noodles in a saucepan of boiling water and simmer for 10 minutes (spaghetti for about 10–12 minutes). Drain.

◆ Divide the hot noodles into 4–6 large heated rice bowls. Sprinkle evenly with the spring onion. Add a large spoonful of the peanut butter and sesame mixture to each bowl of noodles. Pour 15 ml/1 tbsp of soya sauce and vinegar mixture over the contents of each bowl.

Above: Dolmades

DOLMADES

Use fresh vine leaves if they are available. Choose young, tender leaves of a good size. Wash and drain them well, then trim the tough stems with scissors. Boil the leaves in salted water for about 15 minutes, then drain and rinse under cold running water.

SERVES 10–12

30 vine leaves in brine, rinsed well	600 ml/1 pt plus 45 ml/3 tbsp water
50 ml/2 fl oz olive oil	4 tbsp chopped fresh dill
1 large onion, very finely chopped	4 tbsp chopped fresh parsley
125 g/4 oz long-grain rice	2 tbsp chopped fresh mint
2 garlic cloves, crushed	salt and freshly ground black
50 g/2 oz pine kernels	pepper, to taste
50 g/2 oz raisins	1 egg, beaten
1 tsp ground cumin	juice of 1 lemon

◆ Fill a large saucepan with water and bring to a rolling boil. Drop the vine leaves into the water and cook for 3–5 minutes, or until softened. Drain well and set aside.

◆ Heat 30 ml/2 tbsp olive oil in a large frying pan and sauté the onion for 3–5 minutes, or until softened. Add the rice and cook for a further 3–5 minutes, or until lightly coloured, stirring continuously with a wooden spoon. Add the garlic, pine kernels, raisins and cumin and stir in 300 ml/½ pt water. Cover and simmer for about 10 minutes, or until the rice is tender and the liquid has been absorbed. Set aside to cool.

◆ Stir the herbs into the rice mixture and season with salt and pepper. Stir in 15 ml/1 tbsp olive oil and the beaten egg.

◆ Place the remaining olive oil in a large saucepan with 45 ml/ 3 tbsp water. Line the base of the saucepan with 3–4 vine leaves. (You can use any that are torn or otherwise imperfect for this.) To stuff the remaining vine leaves, place about 1 tsp of the rice mixture in the centre of each leaf and neatly fold the leaf around the filling to encase it completely.

◆ Place the stuffed vine leaf in the base of the saucepan, seam-side down, and repeat with the remaining vine leaves, layering them on top of each other neatly. Sprinkle over the lemon juice and about 300 ml/½ pt of water. Place a plate, upside-down, on top of the dolmades to keep them in position during cooking. Cover with a lid and simmer for about 2 hours, or until the vine leaves are tender and the rice is cooked through. Serve warm or cold.

VEGETARIAN SPECIAL FRIED RICE

SERVES 4–6

4–6 dried Chinese mushrooms	2 eggs
1 green sweet pepper, cored and seeded	2 spring onions, finely chopped
	2 tsp salt
1 red sweet pepper, cored and seeded	60–75 ml/4–5 tbsp oil
	1 kg/2 lb cooked rice
125 g/4 oz canned bamboo shoots, drained	15 ml/1 tbsp light soya sauce (optional)

◆ Soak the dried mushrooms in warm water for 25–30 minutes, squeeze dry and discard the hard stalks. Cut the mushrooms into small cubes. Cut the green and red peppers and the bamboo shoots into small cubes. Lightly beat the eggs with about half of the spring onions and a pinch of the salt.

◆ Heat about 30 ml/2 tbsp oil in a hot wok, add the beaten eggs and scramble until set. Remove. Heat the remaining oil. When hot, add the rest of the spring onions followed by all the vegetables and stir-fry until each piece is covered with oil. Add the cooked rice and salt and stir to separate each grain of rice. Finally add the soya sauce if using, blend everything together and serve.

INDIAN

MIXED VEGETABLE BHAJI

The best thing about this dish is that every time it is cooked it has a new taste as the combination of the five vegetables is somehow never quite the same. It is also a very simple and quick way of making a Bhaji.

SERVES 4

125 g/4 oz green beans	30 ml/2 tbsp oil
175 g/6 oz potatoes	7–8 cloves garlic, finely chopped
125 g/4 oz carrots	½ tsp chilli powder
175 g/6 oz aubergine	¼ tsp turmeric powder
125 g/4 oz tomatoes	½–¾ tsp salt
1–2 green chillies	2–3 tbsp mint or coriander leaves

◆ Top and tail and de-string the beans, then chop them into bite-size lengths. Cut the potatoes into quarters and halve them again, preferably leaving the skin on. Scrape and dice the carrots. Cut the aubergine into 4 strips lengthwise and then slice across into 1 cm/½ in chunks. Roughly chop the tomatoes and green chillies.

◆ Measure the oil into a medium-sized heavy saucepan over a medium heat. Add the garlic, stirring it as soon as it begins to turn translucent, then add all the vegetables. Also stir in the chilli powder, turmeric and salt. Mix the spices together thoroughly. Lower the heat, cover the pan and continue to cook for another 20–25 minutes.

◆ Add the mint or coriander leaves, stir and switch the heat off. Let it stand for 2–3 minutes before serving.

PIGEON PEAS AND RICE

This dish is eaten on many of the islands. In the Bahamas it's called, appropriately enough, Bahamian Pigeon Peas and Rice. In Puerto Rico, it's called arroz con gandules – or the same minus the "Bahamian". If you can't find pigeon peas, substitute red beans, preferably small red kidney beans. This dish is great with chicken or any meat and can make a one-dish meal if leftover bits of meat are added.

SERVES 4

30 ml/2 tbsp oil	450 g/1 lb can pigeon peas, drained
1 small onion, chopped	200 g/7 oz long-grain white rice
2 cloves garlic, crushed	450 ml/16 fl oz water
60 ml/4 tbsp tomato purée	30 ml/2 tbsp lime juice
2 ripe tomatoes, chopped	hot pepper sauce to taste
1 green sweet pepper, chopped	salt and freshly ground black pepper
½ tsp thyme	to taste
4 tbsp chopped fresh coriander	

◆ Heat the oil in a saucepan and add the onion. Cook gently for 5 minutes then add the garlic and tomato purée, chopped ripe tomatoes, green sweet pepper and thyme. Cook for another minute. Add the coriander, pigeon peas and rice and sauté for 1 minute. Add the water and lime juice and cook gently, covered, for 15 minutes until the rice is cooked. Add hot pepper sauce, salt and pepper to taste, and serve.

SHANGHAI VEGETABLE RICE

SERVES 5–6

400 g/14 oz long-grain rice	30 ml/2 tbsp vegetable oil
450 g/1 lb green cabbage or spring greens	20 g/¾ oz lard
1½ tbsp dried shrimps	1½ tsp salt
about 225 g/8 oz Chinese sausages	

◆ Wash and measure the rice. Simmer in the same volume of water for 6 minutes. Remove from the heat and leave to stand, covered, for 7–8 minutes.

◆ Wash and dry the cabbage. Chop into 4 × 7.5 cm/1½ × 3 in pieces, removing the tougher stalks. Soak the dried shrimps in hot water to cover for 7–8 minutes, then drain. Cut the sausages slantwise into 2.5 cm/1 in sections.

◆ Heat the oil and lard in a deep saucepan. When hot, stir-fry the shrimps for 30 seconds. Add the cabbage and toss and turn for 1½ minutes until well coated with oil. Sprinkle the cabbage with the salt. Pack in the rice. Push pieces of sausage into the rice. Add 60–75 ml/4–5 tbsp water down the side of the pan. Cover and simmer very gently for about 15 minutes. Transfer to a heated serving dish.

The Baker's Oven

From the ovens of the world come a variety of breads, biscuits and tarts to fill your kitchen with the smell of baking. Try Olive Bread from Greece, Cottage Cheese Bacon Bread from Lithuania, Coconut Bread from the Caribbean. Bread is no longer just the basis of a sandwich!

CLASSIC OLIVE BREAD

*The olives in this bread are sometimes added unpitted. For an
extra-luxurious finish, brush the bread with some beaten egg yolk
15 minutes before the end of the cooking time.*

MAKES 1 LOAF

850 g/1¾ lb strong plain flour
1 tbsp baking powder
pinch of salt
175 ml/6 fl oz water
50 ml/2 fl oz olive oil plus extra for
    greasing

1 tbsp dried mint
1 onion, finely chopped
375 g/12 oz olives, pitted, rinsed and
    dried
1 egg yolk, beaten, to glaze

◆ Preheat the oven to 190°C/375°F/Gas Mark 5. Sift the flour,
baking powder and salt together in a large mixing bowl and make a
well in the centre.

◆ Pour the water into the well with the olive oil, dried mint,
chopped onion and the olives. Stir well with a wooden spoon to
form a stiff dough. Turn the mixture out on to a lightly floured work
surface and knead the dough for at least 10 minutes until smooth
and soft. Return to the cleaned bowl, cover with clingfilm and leave
to rest for about 10 minutes.

◆ Turn the dough out once more on to a lightly floured work
surface. Knead and shape into a 24 cm/9½ in round. Lightly oil a
25 cm/10 in pie dish and place the dough in it. Bake for about
50 minutes, brushing the surface of the bread with the beaten egg
yolk 15 minutes before the end of the cooking time. Transfer the
bread to a wire rack to cool before serving.

PRETZEL-SHAPED SWEET BREAD

This much-loved sweet bread makes a delicious accompaniment to tea drawn from a silver samovar. Given a more cake-like consistency with the addition of more flour and eggs, but retaining the same shape, it is also popular as the centrepiece for a birthday or name-day celebration.

MAKES 1 LOAF

45 ml/3 tbsp lukewarm water
2½ tsp (1 × 8 g/¼ oz packet) active dry yeast
40 g/1½ oz plus 1 tsp sugar
350 g/12 oz plain flour
½ tsp salt

50 g/2 oz unsalted butter
3 standard-size eggs
120 ml/4 fl oz single cream
50 g/2 oz slivered blanched almonds
15 g/½ oz icing sugar

◆ Place the lukewarm water in a small bowl and sprinkle in the yeast and 1 tsp sugar. Leave for 10 minutes to become foamy and almost double in volume.

◆ Sift 300 g/11 oz of the flour, the remaining sugar and the salt into another bowl. Cut in the butter in small pieces, and work the mixture with your hands until it becomes crumbly. Lightly beat 2 eggs and stir into the flour mixture, followed by the cream and the yeast mixture. Combine thoroughly to make a dough. If the dough is not firm enough sift in the remaining flour, little by little.

◆ Gather the dough into a ball and transfer to a well-floured surface. Knead for about 5 minutes, or until it is smooth and elastic. Reshape into a ball, transfer to a lightly buttered bowl, turning to coat in the butter, cover with a tea towel, and let it rise for 30 minutes or until double in size.

◆ Knock down the dough and, on a floured surface, shape it into a long rope about 5 cm/2 in in diameter. Taper the ends and twist the dough over and under into a pretzel shape.

◆ Preheat the oven to 200°C/400°F/Gas Mark 6. Transfer the dough to a buttered baking tray, cover again with the tea towel and leave to rise in a warm place until it has doubled in size, about 30 minutes. Brush with an egg wash made from beating the remaining egg with a little water, and sprinkle with the almonds.

◆ Bake for 15 minutes then cover with foil and bake for 10–15 minutes more, until the top and almonds are golden. Transfer the bread to a rack and when cool sprinkle with sifted icing sugar.

GREEK

CHRISTMAS BREAD

MAKES 2 LOAVES

3 tbsp dried yeast
375 g/12 oz caster sugar
1.6 kg/3½ lb plain flour
pinch of salt
120 ml/4 fl oz warm water
5 eggs
375 ml/12 fl oz milk
few drops of vanilla essence
225 g/8 oz butter, melted

125 g/4 oz dried figs, chopped
50 g/2 oz semi-dried apricots,
    chopped
225 g/8 oz blanched almonds,
    chopped
125 g/4 oz sultanas
finely grated zest of 1 orange
finely grated zest of 1 lemon
vegetable oil, for greasing

◆ Place the yeast, 1 tsp sugar, 2 tbsp flour, salt and warm water into a small bowl. Stir to dissolve the yeast and sugar, then cover with clingfilm and leave in a warm place for about 15 minutes, or until frothy.

◆ In a large mixing bowl, beat together 4 eggs, the remaining sugar and the milk. Stir in the frothy yeast mixture, 750 g/1½ lb of the remaining flour and the vanilla essence. Stir in the melted butter and then the remaining ingredients.

◆ Mix to form a stiff dough, then turn out on to a lightly floured surface and knead, with the addition of the remaining flour if necessary, for about 10 minutes or until the dough is smooth.

◆ Return the dough to the cleaned mixing bowl and cover with clingfilm. Leave in a warm place to prove for about 1½ hours or until doubled in size. Turn out on to a lightly floured surface and knead the dough back to its original size. Return to the bowl again, cover, and leave in a warm place for a further 30 minutes.

◆ Divide the dough into 6 equal portions. Roll each portion into about a 30 cm/12 in sausage shape and braid 3 of them together to form a plait, moulding the ends together to seal. Repeat with the other 3 sausage shapes to make another plait. Place each braid on a lightly oiled baking sheet, cover loosely with clingfilm and leave in a warm place for a final 30–40 minutes until the bread has risen.

◆ Preheat the oven to 180°C/350°F/Gas Mark 4. Beat the remaining egg in a small bowl and use to glaze both braids. Bake the bread for about 30 minutes, or until golden and hollow-sounding when tapped underneath. Transfer to a wire rack to cool for serving.

CAJUN

SWEET-POTATO AND PECAN MUFFINS

MAKES 15–24

175 g/6 oz plain flour
75 g/3 oz wholewheat flour
75 g/3 oz oat bran
1¼ tsp baking powder
¾ tsp baking soda
½ tsp salt
275 g/10 oz light brown sugar
1½ tsp ground cinnamon

¾ tsp grated nutmeg
1 tsp grated lemon zest
75 ml/5 tbsp vegetable oil
3 eggs, lightly beaten
175 ml/6 fl oz water
350 g/12 oz sweet potato pulp
150 g/5 oz coarsely chopped pecans

◆ Preheat the oven to 200°C/400°F/Gas Mark 6. Lightly grease 2 muffin tins. Mix all the dry ingredients together.

◆ In a small bowl, combine the oil, eggs, water and sweet potato. Add to the dry ingredients and mix by hand, stirring only until the ingredients are well blended. Stir in the pecans. Spoon into the muffin tins. Bake until a cocktail stick inserted in the centre comes out clean, 24–27 minutes.

PECAN CRESCENT ROLLS

These crescent rolls, made with a yeast dough and a sweet pecan filling, are irresistible served warm.

MAKES 24–32 ROLLS

Dough
1 package (4 g/¼ oz) active dry
    yeast
75 g/3 oz caster sugar
120 ml/4 fl oz water, heated to
    40–50°C/105–115°F
2 eggs, lightly beaten
120 ml/4 fl oz double cream
15 ml/3 fl oz melted unsalted butter

1 tsp salt
425 g/15 oz plain flour

Filling
120 ml/4 fl oz melted unsalted butter
225 g/8 oz light brown sugar
4 tsp cinnamon
100 g/4 oz pecans, finely chopped

◆ To make the dough, combine the yeast, 1 tsp sugar and water in a small bowl or measuring cup. Let it stand until the yeast foams and forms a head, about 10 minutes. If the yeast does not foam, it won't rise. Make sure the water is the right temperature. If it's too cold, it won't activate the yeast, and if it's too hot, it will kill it.

◆ While the yeast is proving, combine the eggs, cream, remaining sugar, butter and salt. Stir in the yeast mixture. Add the flour, 125 g/4 oz at a time, and mix. After you have added 350 g/12 oz

flour, begin kneading with your hands. Add 1–2 tbsp flour at a time, as needed, when all the previous flour is incorporated and the dough gets sticky. Knead until smooth and elastic, 8–10 minutes.

◆ Put the dough in an oiled bowl and turn by hand several times until it is coated. Cover with a dishcloth and stand in a warm place until doubled in bulk, about 1½ hours.

◆ Meanwhile, make the filling. Make a paste of the melted butter, sugar and cinnamon, then mix in the pecans.

◆ Punch down the dough and cut in half. Roll out each half into a circle about 38 cm/15 in in diameter on a floured surface. Cut each circle into 12–16 wedges, so it looks like a wheel with spokes.

◆ Spread half of the filling on each circle, putting more towards the outside of the circle than in the middle. Beginning at the outside edge, roll up each wedge and turn the ends in slightly so each roll resembles a crescent. Put the rolls on greased baking sheets, cover with tea towels and put in a warm place to rise, about 1½ hours.

◆ Preheat the oven to 190°C/375°F/Gas Mark 5. Bake the rolls for 12–15 minutes, watching carefully: the sugar that oozes out of the filling can burn easily, ruining the taste of the rolls.

EASY CINNAMON BALLS

MAKES ABOUT 20

225 g/8 oz finely ground blanched
    almonds or walnuts
200 g/7 oz sugar
1 tbsp ground cinnamon

2 egg whites
⅛ tsp cream of tartar
icing sugar and cinnamon for rolling

◆ Preheat the oven to 160°C/325°F/Gas Mark 3. Lightly grease a
large biscuit tray. In a medium bowl, combine the ground almonds
or walnuts, half the sugar and the cinnamon. Set aside.

◆ In another medium bowl, with an electric mixer, beat the egg
whites until frothy. Add the cream of tartar and continue beating
until soft peaks form. Gradually add the remaining sugar, 15 g/½ oz
at a time, beating well after each addition, until the whites are stiff
and glossy. Gently fold in the nut mixture.

◆ With wet hands, shape the mixture into walnut-size balls. Place
on the biscuit tray about 2.5 cm/1 in apart. Bake until golden brown
and set, 25–30 minutes. Remove the biscuit tray to a wire rack to
cool slightly.

◆ In a small bowl, combine 50 g/2 oz icing sugar and ¼ tsp
cinnamon until well blended. Roll each warm ball in the mixture to
coat, then set on a wire rack to cool completely. Add more icing
sugar and cinnamon if necessary. When cold, roll each ball again in
the sugar mixture.

> NOTE: If you find the mixture too soft to roll, add a little more
> ground almond or a little fine matzo meal to stiffen it.

SWEET POT-CHEESE TARTLETS

*These are served as a savoury snack, as a sweet to go with tea, as
here, or as a large dessert tart.*

MAKES ABOUT 16 TARTLETS

200 g/7 oz plain flour
½ tsp baking powder
50 g/2 oz sugar
pinch of salt
1 large egg
90 ml/3 fl oz sour cream
65 g/2½ oz unsalted butter

Filling
50 ml/2 fl oz rum

30 ml/2 tbsp water
75 g/3 oz raisins
500 g/18 oz cottage cheese
4 eggs
175 g/6 oz sugar
2 tsp grated lemon zest
125 g/4 oz clarified butter, melted
¼ tsp salt
50 g/2 oz flour

◆ Make the filling first. Heat the rum and water in a saucepan over
high heat until almost boiling. Remove from the heat and stir in the
raisins. Set aside.

◆ Line a colander with muslin and pour in the cottage cheese.
Leave to drain for 3 hours.

◆ In a large bowl, beat the cottage cheese using an electric mixer.
Beat in the eggs, one at a time, and the sugar, until the mixture is
pale in colour. Stir in the lemon zest, melted butter, salt and flour,
1 tbsp at a time. Drain the raisins, discard the liquid and fold the
raisins into the cottage cheese.

◆ To make the dough, sift the flour, baking powder, sugar and salt
into a large bowl. Beat the egg, sour cream and butter in a small
bowl. Make a well in the centre of the flour and pour the egg
mixture into it. With your hands, slowly work the flour into the
liquid, then beat until the mixture forms a ball. Wrap in clingfilm
and chill for 1 hour.

◆ Preheat the oven to 200°C/400°F/Gas Mark 6. On a well floured
surface, roll the dough out into a rectangle as thinly as possible. Cut
out 16 or so 10 cm/4 in rounds from the dough, gathering and re-
rolling the scraps as necessary. Make a rim around each circle by
folding over and pinching up the dough, so that you end up with
shallow tartlet cases.

◆ Place the cases on a greased baking tray and spoon some of the
filling into each case. Bake for 15–20 minutes, or until the tartlets
are golden. Remove and cool on a wire rack.

Above: Sweet Pot-Cheese Tartlets

BAKES

These are the Creole version of a scone, fried in hot oil, and variations of this recipe are eaten throughout the islands. Make a big batch — they go fast!

225 g/8 oz plain flour	2 tsp baking powder
25 g/1 oz butter	2 tsp sugar
½ tsp salt	150 ml/¼ pt milk

◆ Sift the dry ingredients into a bowl, then cut in the butter with a knife until the mixture resembles breadcrumbs. Pour in the milk and stir to make a soft dough. Knead on a floured board for about 5 minutes, then refrigerate for 30 minutes. Break the dough into lemon-sized pieces, roll into balls and flatten to 1 cm/½ in thickness. Fry these in hot oil until golden.

LITHUANIAN

COTTAGE CHEESE BACON BREAD

Cottage cheese and honey are commonly used as baking ingredients in Lithuania. This recipe mixes wholemeal and white flour to give a hint of the sturdy type of bread found in the Baltic States.

MAKES 1 LOAF

50 ml/2 fl oz vegetable oil	1 egg
175 g/6 oz lean bacon, finely chopped	175 g/6 oz cottage cheese
2 heaped tbsp finely chopped spring onion	150 g/5 oz wholewheat flour
50 ml/2 fl oz honey	150 g/5 oz strong white flour
175 ml/6 fl oz milk	2 tsp baking powder
	½ tsp baking soda
	scant tsp salt

◆ In a small saucepan, heat the vegetable oil over medium-high heat. Add the bacon and fry for a few minutes until the bacon is cooked. Turn down the heat and stir in the spring onion, allowing it to wilt slightly. Then add the honey, heat through, and remove from the hob. Beat in the milk, egg, and then the cottage cheese. Blend thoroughly and set aside.

◆ In a large bowl, sift together the two flours, baking powder and soda and the salt. Make a well and pour in the cottage cheese mixture, beating gently — do not overbeat.

◆ Preheat the oven to 190°C/375°F/Gas Mark 5. Scrape the bread dough into a buttered and floured 23 × 13 × 7.5 cm/9 × 5 × 3 in loaf tin. Flatten the top of the loaf with a spatula and drop the loaf sharply twice on a hard surface to eliminate air pockets. Bake for 45–50 minutes, or until the top is golden brown.

◆ Place the tin on a wire rack to cool for 15 minutes before turning out. Cool completely before serving.

CHEESE-FILLED BREADS

MAKES ABOUT 16–18

65 g/2½ oz unsalted butter, softened
120 ml/4 fl oz lukewarm water
2½ tsp (1 × 8 g/¼ oz packet) active
    dry yeast
2 tsp sugar
275 g/10 oz plain flour

1 tsp salt
450 g/1 lb halloumi cheese, grated
2 eggs
2 tbsp finely chopped oregano,
    marjoram or tarragon

◆ In a small saucepan, heat 45 g/1½ oz butter over a low heat until only just melted. Allow to cool.

◆ Place the water in a small bowl and sprinkle the yeast and sugar into it. Leave for 15 minutes in a warm place, or until foamy. In a large bowl, mix together 225 g/8 oz flour and the salt. Make a well in the centre and pour in the yeast and the melted butter; stir with a fork until you have a pliable dough.

◆ Transfer the dough to a floured surface and knead with your hands for 5 minutes, adding the remaining flour as you work the dough. When the dough is no longer sticky but smooth and still soft, transfer it to a well-buttered bowl and turn it to coat with the butter. Leave it to rise in a warm place, covered with clingfilm, for about 1 hour, or until doubled in size.

◆ In another bowl, stir together the grated cheese, 1 egg and the remaining softened butter. Work the mixture well with your hands and set aside.

◆ Knock back the dough, halve it and roll one half into a 40 × 20 cm/16 × 8 in rectangle. Divide the rectangle into squares. Use half the cheese mixture to make mounds in the centre of the squares and fold the sides up around and slightly over the mixture, pulling out the corners slightly. Repeat with remaining dough and cheese mixture.

◆ Preheat the oven to 190°C/375°F/Gas Mark 5. Make an egg wash by mixing the remaining egg with a little water in a small bowl. Arrange the filled bread cases on two baking trays and brush with the egg wash. Allow them to rest for 15 minutes in a warm place, then bake in the oven for 20–25 minutes, or until they are golden and the cheese is toasted. Transfer to a rack, sprinkle with the fresh herbs and leave to cool for 15 minutes before serving warm. (The breads may be frozen and reheated at the same temperature for 25 minutes from frozen.)

COCONUT BREAD

This is so nice for breakfast or tea with any jam, jelly, or marmalade – or spread a little cream cheese on a slice and then top with jam or marmalade! Slice a couple of the extra loaves thickly, wrap and freeze, and you'll have a ready supply to pop in the toaster. These will keep for a couple of months.

MAKES 4 LOAVES

450 g/1 lb butter, softened
450 g/1 lb sugar
8 eggs
8 tsp coconut essence
1 litre/1¾ pt sour cream

450 g/1 lb desiccated coconut
1 kg/2 lb plain flour
4 tsp bicarbonate of soda
4 tsp baking powder

◆ Preheat the oven to 180°C/350°F/Gas Mark 4. Cream together the butter and sugar. Beat in the eggs and coconut essence, then the sour cream. Add the coconut. Stir together the flour, bicarbonate of soda and baking powder and beat into a batter. Divide between 4 lightly greased loaf tins and bake for about 45 minutes, or until a cocktail stick inserted in the centre comes out without any clinging batter or wet crumbs. Leave to cool before turning out.

SWEET CARAWAY BISCUITS

These sweet biscuits exhibit the Latvian love of caraway, even in sweet things.

MAKES ABOUT 48

125 g/4 oz unsalted butter, softened
225 g/8 oz sugar
1 egg
2 tsp caraway seeds

juice and grated zest of 1 small
    orange
300 g/11 oz plain flour
½ tsp baking soda
¼ tsp salt

◆ In a bowl, cream the butter with the sugar until light yellow and fluffy. Stir in the egg, caraway seeds, orange zest and 30 ml/2 tbsp of the juice. Combine thoroughly.

◆ Sift the flour, baking soda and salt into a bowl and slowly stir into the butter mixture until you have a cohesive dough. Remove the dough from the bowl and place on a 30 cm/12 in long piece of greaseproof paper. Form the dough into a rough sausage and roll back and forth, wrapped in the paper, until the sausage is smooth and has become about 25 cm/10 in long and 5 cm/2 in wide. Wrap well in the paper and foil and freeze until solid.

◆ Preheat the oven to 180°C/350°F/Gas Mark 4. Cut the sausage into 1.5 cm/¼ in slices and bake for 10–12 minutes, until the edges are golden brown.

Desserts

The more hot and spicy the main course, the more cooling the dessert. Many tropical dishes consist simply of fruit, milk, ice cream and yoghurt. Now's the time to make good use of all the wonderful fruit on display in our shops.

PEARS IN HONEY SAUCE

SERVES 6

6 firm, ripe pears
60 ml/4 tbsp runny honey
60 ml/4 tbsp sweet liqueur, eg
    Chinese Rose Dew, kirsch, cherry
    brandy

50 g/2 oz sugar
30 ml/2 tbsp water

◆ Peel the pears, leaving on the stalks and a little of the surrounding skin. Blend the honey with the liqueur, 50 g/2 oz sugar and the water.

◆ Stand the pears in a flat-bottomed pan and barely cover with water. Bring slowly to the boil. Add the remaining sugar and simmer gently for 20 minutes. Refrigerate the pears with a quarter of the sugar water for 2 hours, discarding the remaining sugar water.

◆ Stand each pear in a small bowl. Spoon over a little sugar water, then pour about 30 ml/2 tbsp of the honey sauce over each pear. Chill for another 30 minutes before serving.

KHIR WITH ORANGES

SERVES 4

1.2 litres/2 pt milk
40 g/1½ oz sugar

2 oranges, peeled

◆ Boil the milk in a large saucepan, stirring constantly. Add the sugar and stir. Reduce the heat and, stirring occasionally, simmer until it is reduced to 450 ml/¾ pt. Cool.

◆ Remove all the pith from the oranges and slice. Add to the cooled milk. Serve chilled.

FRIED SWEETS IN SYRUP

SERVES 4

150 g/5 oz plain flour
½ tsp baking powder
milk
275 g/10 oz sugar

250 ml/8 fl oz water
few drops yellow food colouring
few drops rose water
oil for deep frying

◆ Sieve together the flour and baking powder. Add enough milk to make a thick batter of pouring consistency. Keep the batter in a warm place overnight.

◆ When you are ready to fry the sweets, prepare the syrup. Place the sugar and water in a large saucepan and bring to a boil. Boil for 5–6 minutes until the syrup becomes slightly thick. Remove from the heat and add the yellow food colouring and rose water. Stir well and keep aside.

◆ Heat the oil over a medium high heat. Place the batter in a piping bag with a 5 mm/¼ in plain nozzle. Squeeze the batter into the hot oil, making spiral shapes of about 6 cm/2½ in in diameter.

◆ Fry until golden. Drain and add to the syrup for 1 minute. Remove from the syrup.

CRÈME BRÛLÉE ICE-CREAM

Custards are a basic part of Spanish cuisine in every region. The best of them, crème brûlée, may well have been invented in Catalonia. There it is served as a flat saucer of custard with the caramel lying in a net across it. This is done with a quemadora, a red-hot iron held over it, or under a big grill in restaurants, but is more difficult to manage without them. The ice-cream is easier, and popular too, for it is very rich.

SERVES 6

500 ml/18 fl oz creamy milk (or 1:1 milk and single cream)	125 g/4 oz caster sugar
	4 egg yolks
3 strips lemon zest	1 tsp cornflour
1 cinnamon stick	50 g/2 oz demerara sugar
	30 ml/2 tbsp water

◆ Bring the milk to a simmer with the lemon zest, cinnamon stick and caster sugar, stirring gently. Turn off the heat and leave to infuse for 20 minutes.

◆ Beat the egg yolks and cornflour with a wooden spoon in a bowl that fits over a pan of simmering water. Strain the hot milk into the egg mixture. Stir over simmering water until the custard coats the back of the spoon. Pour into a small bread tin, cool and then freeze for 2 hours.

◆ Without special equipment it is easiest to make caramel in a small saucepan. Put in the demerara sugar and water and heat until it smells of caramel. Then, without hesitating, pour it onto a sheet of foil laid over a board. Wait until it has set and when it is hard, snap it up and grind (though not too uniformly) in a blender or food processor.

◆ Remove the custard ice-cream from the freezer and beat well with a fork. Stir 3 tbsp caramel into the ice-cream and freeze until firm. Soften in the fridge for 30 minutes and sprinkle with the remaining caramel before serving.

INDIAN

ICE CREAM WITH ALMONDS AND PISTACHIO NUTS (KULFI)

SERVES 6

1.2 litres/2 pt milk
50 g/2 oz sugar
2 tbsp ground almonds

2 tbsp pistachio nuts, skinned and chopped
few drops rose water

◆ Bring the milk to a boil, stirring constantly. Lower the heat and simmer, stirring occasionally, until it reduces to about 500 ml/ 18 fl oz.

◆ Add the sugar and mix thoroughly. Continue to simmer for another 2–3 minutes. Remove from the heat and let it cool completely.

◆ Add the almonds and mix into the thickened milk, making sure no lumps form. Then stir in the pistachio nuts and rose water.

◆ Place the mixture in a dish, cover it with its own lid or aluminium foil and place it in the freezer.

◆ Take it out of the freezer after 20 minutes and give it a good stir to break up the ice crystals. Repeat twice more.

◆ After this, it may be divided up into 6 chilled individual dishes and covered and frozen for about 4–5 hours. Take it out of the freezer about 10 minutes before you are ready to serve.

VIETNAMESE

COCONUT ICE CREAM

SERVES 4

275 ml/10 fl oz thick coconut milk
350 ml/12 fl oz fresh cream
2 eggs
2 egg yolks
5 ml/1 tsp vanilla essence
125 g/4 oz sugar

salt

To garnish
50 g/2 oz desiccated coconut, dry-fried until golden brown
sprigs of mint

◆ Heat the coconut milk and cream over a medium heat and cook for 5 minutes without boiling over. Beat together the eggs, egg yolks, vanilla, sugar and salt.

◆ Place a deep bowl in a saucepan with boiling water up to the halfway mark of the bowl. Pour in the egg mixture and beat in the warm coconut milk mixture, a little at a time. Stir until the mixture thickens enough to coat a spoon. Remove from the heat, stirring occasionally as it cools.

◆ Pour into a bowl when it is cool enough to be put into the freezer. Freeze for 1 hour. Scoop out into a blender or food processor and process until smooth. Pour back into the bowl and freeze until solid.

◆ Serve in scoops, garnished attractively with desiccated coconut and sprigs of mint.

LEBANESE

STUFFED DATES

MAKES 12

12 plump fresh dates
125 g/4 oz ricotta cheese
1 tsp caster sugar

1 tsp finely grated fresh lemon zest
12 whole almonds

◆ Carefully slit the dates and remove the pits; gently open up the hole created. Set aside.

◆ In a bowl, combine thoroughly the cheese, sugar and lemon zest. Divide the mixture between the 12 dates, pushing it into the cavities and moulding the dates around the filling. Push an almond into the top of each date. Arrange the dates attractively on a small serving plate.

Above: Stuffed Dates

FLAN

"Flan" is a baked caramel-topped custard. It can be made with condensed milk, which is what most modern Mexican working people use.

SERVES 6–10

275 g/9 oz sugar	6 large egg yolks
2 litres/3½ pt milk	1 tsp vanilla essence
6–8 large eggs	

◆ Add 225 g/8 oz sugar to the milk and bring to the boil. Reduce the milk to half its original volume, stirring regularly as it simmers. This takes about 45 minutes.

◆ In a heavy non-stick saucepan, melt the remaining sugar. Holding the pan above the flame, shake constantly. Slowly, the sugar will form into clumps, then melt to a uniform dark honey-brown. Pour this into a metal pie dish, and roll it around to coat the inside. (Before adding the caramel you can brush the inside of the dish with a cooking oil or butter it lightly to prevent sticking.) If you are making individual flans you will need to melt two or three times as much sugar to coat the interiors of all of the pie dishes. Let the caramel cool to room temperature.

◆ Beat the whole eggs, yolks and vanilla essence together until smooth and uniform. Slowly, beat in the hot reduced milk. Strain into mould(s), and allow to cool to room temperature.

◆ Preheat the oven to 175°C/350°F/Gas Mark 4. Stand the mould(s) in a roasting tin containing about 5–7.5 cm/2–3 in of water to prevent burning. Cook in the oven until the custard is just set – about 30 minutes for individual flans, or 45 minutes for one large one.

◆ For the best chance of releasing the flan unbroken, chill it thoroughly and run a very thin knife around the edge – a very narrow palette knife is ideal. Go all the way to the bottom of the mould. Then, place a plate upside-down on top of the mould, invert, and hope for the best. You should feel a slight shock as the flan comes out and lands on the plate.

MANGO SOUFFLÉ

SERVES 4

2 tsp gelatine
45 ml/3 tbsp water
4 eggs
300 ml/½ pt mango juice or 225 g/
    8 oz mango pulp

2 tsp granulated sugar
salt
25 g/1 oz caster sugar
½ tsp vanilla flavouring

◆ In a small bowl, mix the gelatine with the water.

◆ Separate the eggs, putting the yolks into a mixing bowl. Beat the yolks well and mix thoroughly with the mango juice or pulp.

◆ Stir in the granulated sugar, gelatine and ½ tsp salt.

◆ Put the mixing bowl over a pan of boiling water, taking care that the bowl does not touch the water or the eggs will scramble. Beat the mixture for 10 minutes, then remove from the heat.

◆ Whisk the egg whites with ½ tsp salt and the caster sugar until stiff, then fold into the yolks, adding the vanilla flavouring.

◆ Divide the mixture between 4 small dishes and chill before serving.

SOFT SWEET CHEESE PANCAKES

These hand-formed pancakes are sometimes served for breakfast in the better Moscow and St Petersburg hotels. The combination of lemon rind, eggs and cheese is a favourite throughout Eastern Europe and Western Russia.

SERVES 4–6

50 g/2 oz plain flour
450 g/1 lb curd cheese
1 large egg
salt
15 g/½ oz sugar
½ tsp vanilla essence

grated zest of 1 small lemon
flour for dredging
40–50 g/1½–2 oz butter
sour cream (optional)
fresh fruit – apricots, peaches,
    raspberries, as desired (optional)

◆ Sieve the flour into a large bowl, then force the curd cheese through the same sieve into the bowl. Add the egg, a pinch of salt, the sugar, vanilla essence and lemon zest. Stir to mix well.

◆ Transfer the mixture to a floured board and form into 12 small patties. Arrange the patties on a plate, cover with clingfilm, and chill them for 2–24 hours.

◆ Before cooking, dredge the patties in flour, brushing off the excess. Melt the butter in a frying pan and cook the pancakes until they are golden brown on both sides. Serve warm with sour cream and fresh soft fruit, peeled and sliced, if desired.

INDIAN

PUMPKIN HALVA

SERVES 4

450 g/1 lb pumpkin (preferably white)
600 ml/1 pt milk
150 g/5 oz sugar

1 tsp rose water
125 g/4 oz ghee
¼ tsp ground cardamom seeds
10–15 cashew nuts, halved

◆ Scrape the seeds and stringy bits from the inside of the pumpkin, cut the flesh from the skin and chop into chunks.

◆ Grate the pumpkin coarsely, put in a muslin cloth and squeeze out all the moisture.

◆ Put the pumpkin in a pan with the milk, sugar and rose water and cook over a low heat for 30 minutes or more, stirring briskly, until all the milk has evaporated.

◆ Stir in the ghee and continue cooking until it separates. Drain off any butter not absorbed by the pumpkin mixture.

◆ Stir in the cardamom and cashew nuts and spread the mixture in a greased dish with straight sides, in one layer about 5 cm/2 in deep.

◆ Leave for about 45 minutes until set, then cut into squares.

PEACH-AMARETTO ICE CREAM

W hat a delicious way to celebrate summer! This ice cream is made with a rich custard base and juicy, sweet, fresh peaches. Frozen ones will do in a pinch, but they are not as good. You'll need Amaretti, the light, crunchy Italian biscuits made with egg whites and almond. You'll also need an ice-cream maker with a 1.75 litre/3 pt capacity.

SERVES 6 – 8

350 ml/12 fl oz double cream
350 ml/12 fl oz whole milk
3 egg yolks
225 g/8 oz caster sugar
1 tsp vanilla essence
1.75 kg/4 lb fresh peaches, peeled,
    stoned and chopped

15 ml/1 tbsp Amaretto liqueur or
    5 ml/1 tsp almond essence
25 g/1 oz Amaretti biscuits, coarsely
    chopped

◆ In a medium saucepan, bring the cream and milk to a boil. Remove from the heat, then leave to cool for 10 minutes.

◆ In a small bowl, beat the egg yolks until frothy. Add the sugar and continue beating until the mixture is pale yellow. Add a few spoonfuls of the warm cream to the eggs to raise their temperature gently without scrambling them. Add a few more spoonfuls of cream, then whisk the egg mixture into the rest of the cream. Cook over a medium heat, just until the custard thickens slightly, but do not boil. Remove from heat and stir in the vanilla essence. Chill for at least 30 minutes or for several hours.

◆ Meanwhile, purée the peaches to make 475 ml/16 fl oz thick, chunky pulp. Add Amaretto or almond essence and set aside for 1 hour or so.

◆ Put the cold custard and peach purée into an ice-cream maker. If your machine allows you to add ingredients easily later, wait until the ice cream is partially churned before adding the chopped Amaretti. Otherwise, add it now. Churn according to manufacturer's directions. Freeze until ready to serve.

TOFFEE APPLES

SERVES 4

3 apples
15 ml/1 tbsp lemon juice
125 g/4 oz cornflour
2 tbsp sesame seeds
450 ml/¾ pt ground nut oil

125 g/4 oz ice cubes
600 ml/1 pt iced water
350 g/12 oz sugar
5 ml/1 tsp vinegar

◆ Peel and core the apples and cut each into 6 pieces. Cut each piece into 3. Sprinkle lemon juice over the apples immediately to prevent discoloration. Coat the apple pieces with cornflour and set them aside. Sauté the sesame seeds in a pan over a low heat. Set aside.

◆ Rub a serving plate with oil and set it aside. Place the ice cubes and iced water in a bowl and set them aside.

◆ Heat the oil and fry the apple for 10 minutes until nicely golden. Remove, drain and set aside. In another pan bring 350 ml/12 fl oz water to a vigorous boil. Add the sugar, stirring until it starts to caramelize, then add the vinegar and stir. Add the apple pieces until they are evenly coated with syrup. Sprinkle sesame seeds over the apple pieces and transfer them to a plate.

◆ Dip the syrup-coated apple pieces into the iced water. Remove immediately or when the syrup hardens and becomes brittle. It is worth practising this recipe a few times to achieve the correct contrast between the brittle, ice-cold coating of caramelized sugar and the hot, tender apple centre.

FRUIT CHAAT

SERVES 4

175 g/6 oz canned guavas, drained
175 g/6 oz honeydew melon
125 g/4 oz pears
125 g/4 oz apple
125 g/4 oz tangerines
¼ tsp cumin seeds, crushed
pinch of chilli powder

pinch of freshly ground black pepper
pinch of salt
2–3 tsp sugar
30 ml/2 tbsp fresh orange juice
10 ml/2 tsp lemon juice
fresh mint leaves, slightly crushed or broken, to garnish

◆ Cut up all the fruits into small cubes or tiny segments so that the spices can mingle into the fruits easily.

◆ Mix all the spices together in a bowl, pour in the sugar and orange and lemon juice, and stir the mixture to blend them. Pour this over the fruit, mix gently, garnish with the mint leaves and chill well before serving.

TOFFEE BANANAS

SERVES 4

4 bananas, peeled
1 egg
15 g/½ oz plain flour

oil for deep-frying
50 g/2 oz sugar
15 ml/1 tbsp cold water

◆ Cut the bananas in half lengthwise and then cut each half into two crosswise.

◆ Beat the egg, add the flour and mix well to make a smooth batter.

◆ Heat the oil in a wok or deep-fryer. Coat each piece of banana with batter and deep fry until golden. Remove and drain.

◆ Pour off the excess oil, leaving about 15 ml/1 tbsp oil in the wok. Add the sugar and water and stir over a medium heat to dissolve the sugar. Continue stirring and when the sugar has caramelized add the hot banana pieces. Coat well and remove. Dip the hot bananas in cold water to harden the toffee and serve immediately.

Above: Fruit Chaat

PLANTANOS

*F*ried or baked plantains (plantanos) are a popular Mexican dessert. If you wish you can use bananas instead.

SERVES 4

4 plantains	½ tsp cinnamon
50 g/2 oz sugar	50 g/2 oz butter, cubed

◆ Preheat the oven to 160°C/325°F/Gas Mark 3. Peel the plantains and cut them in half lengthwise and then in half crosswise. Mix sugar with the cinnamon and dust it over the plantains. Dot the butter cubes over and around the plantains and place them in the oven for 15 minutes until they are softened.

TEA ICE CREAM WITH RUM SAUCE

SERVES 8

125 g/4 oz kumquats, trimmed and finely chopped	350 ml/12 fl oz double cream
125 g/4 oz caster sugar	3 large egg whites
30 ml/2 tbsp water	50 g/2 oz icing sugar
2 tbsp shelled pistachios	
75 ml/3 fl oz boiling water	**Topping**
5 tbsp black tea leaves	15 g/½ oz icing sugar
5 large egg yolks	15 ml/1 tbsp golden rum
	120 ml/4 fl oz cold double cream

◆ In a small saucepan, combine the kumquats with half the caster sugar and the water. Bring to the boil, stirring, then lower the heat and simmer, stirring frequently, until the kumquats are pulpy. Let the mixture cool and drain off the excess liquid.

◆ Pour boiling water over the pistachios and leave for 1 minute. Drain and rub off the skins.

◆ Place the boiling water in a bowl and add 2 tbsp tea leaves. Leave to stand for 3 minutes, then strain into another bowl. Press the leaves with a spoon to extract all the juice.

◆ In a small saucepan, mix together the steeped tea and the remaining caster sugar. Bring to the boil and stir until the sugar is dissolved and the syrup is shiny and thickening, or measures 50°C/120°F on a sugar thermometer.

◆ Beat the egg yolks until thick and lemon-coloured. Pour in the tea syrup little by little, beating constantly, until cooled.

◆ In a saucepan, heat 120 ml/4 fl oz cream until it boils, remove from the heat and stir in the remaining tea leaves. Leave to stand for 5 minutes, then strain into a bowl, pressing hard with the back of a spoon to extract all the juice. Whisk together the tea-cream and the egg yolk mixture.

◆ In another bowl, beat the egg whites until they reach soft peaks, then beat in the icing sugar until they become stiff. Fold the meringue into the tea-cream and egg yolk mixture.

◆ In another bowl, beat the remaining cream until it reaches soft peak stage. Fold into the mixture with the pistachios.

◆ Line a 1.25 litre/2¼ pt bombe mould with clingfilm. Spoon the kumquats into the bottom of the mould, pressing up around the sides as far as they will go. Pour in the tea-cream mixture and smooth the top. Freeze for at least 4 hours, or until solid.

◆ Meanwhile, make the topping. Beat the rum and sugar until the sugar has dissolved. Add the cream and beat until the mixture has thickened. Serve the ice cream with the rum sauce.

TROPICAL FRUIT SALAD

SERVES 4

225 g/8 oz mango flesh
175 g/6 oz honeydew melon
125 g/4 oz kiwi fruit
150 g/5 oz canned lychees

30 ml/2 tbsp orange juice
10 ml/2 tsp lemon juice
15 g/½ oz sugar

◆ Cut the mango into bite-size cubes. Use a melon baller to cut out as many little balls as possible from the melon. Peel and slice the kiwi fruit. Drain the lychees.

◆ Mix the orange and lemon juices and sugar together and pour over the fruit. Mix well and chill.

◆ Just before serving, divide the fruit between 4 serving dishes and top each one with whole lychees.

172

CHINESE

ALMOND JUNKET

This junket can be made from agar-agar, isinglass or gelatine. When chilled and served with a variety of fresh and canned fruit, it is a most refreshing dessert.

SERVES 4

8 g/⅓ oz agar-agar or isinglass or 25 g/1 oz gelatine powder
50 g/2 oz sugar
600 ml/1 pt water

120 ml/4 fl oz evaporated milk
1 tsp almond essence
1 can cherries with syrup to garnish

◆ Dissolve the agar-agar or isinglass and the sugar in the water over gentle heat. (If using gelatine powder, just follow the instructions on the packet.)
◆ Add the milk and almond essence and pour the mixture into a large serving bowl. Allow to cool for at least 30 minutes and then place in the refrigerator for 2–3 hours to set. To serve, cut the junket into small cubes and pour the canned fruit and syrup over it.

INDIAN

FRUIT AND YOGHURT CHAAT

SERVES 4

125 g/4 oz guava
125 g/4 oz pineapple
1 banana
225 g/8 oz natural yoghurt
25–40 g/1–1½ oz sugar
10 ml/2 tsp lemon juice

pinch of rock salt
pinch of freshly ground black pepper
pinch of cardamom pods, crushed, or pinch of grated nutmeg
50 g/2 oz pomegranate, flesh only, or 75 g/3 oz fresh cherries

◆ Cut all the fruit except the pomegranate into bite-size pieces.
◆ Whisk the yoghurt briefly until it is smooth.
◆ Add the sugar, lemon juice, salt, pepper and cardamom or nutmeg to the yoghurt and mix them together well.
◆ Add the fruit to the yoghurt and mix gently. Divide the mixture between 4 serving dishes. Scatter the pomegranate over each dish and chill well before serving.

RUSSIAN

CHARLOTTE RUSSE

SERVES 8–9

15–30 ml/1–2 tbsp apricot jam
16–18 sponge fingers
150 ml/¼ pt whipping or double cream
120 ml/4 fl oz can baby mandarin segments, drained

Custard filling
450 g/1 lb can apricot halves in syrup, drained and syrup reserved

25 ml/5 tsp gelatine
8 egg yolks
125 g/4 oz sugar
300 ml/½ pt milk
175 ml/6 fl oz double cream
120 ml/4 fl oz sour cream
90 ml/6 tbsp Cointreau, Grand Marnier or other orange liqueur

◆ Spread the jam thinly around the inside edge of a deep 20–23 cm/8–9 in springform tin. Measure the biscuits against the sides of the tin and cut off one end so that they will stand up. Line them up side-to-side around the inside of the tin, pressing them into the jam.
◆ Make the purée and custard filling. Place the drained fruit in a blender or a food processor fitted with the metal blade. Add 120 ml/4 fl oz apricot syrup and purée the apricots. Place 45 ml/3 tbsp apricot syrup in a small bowl and sprinkle the gelatine into it. Put the bowl into a pan of hot water and stir the syrup and gelatine until the latter has dissolved.
◆ Beat the egg yolks with the sugar in a bowl placed over a pan of hot water until the mixture is creamy and lemon yellow. Bring the milk to simmering point and slowly stir it into the egg mixture, stirring all the time. Continue to stir over the hot water until the mixture has become a spoon-coating custard. Stir the gelatine into the custard, take the pan off the heat and allow the mixture to cool to room temperature.
◆ Whisk the apricot purée into the custard, then cover and chill in the refrigerator until the mixture is satiny and just beginning to set. In a bowl, combine the double cream and sour cream and whip until they reach stiff peak stage. Fold into the apricot mixture, together with the orange liqueur. Pour the mixture into the biscuit-lined tin. Chill for 4 hours or overnight.
◆ To unmould, run a knife around between the tin and the biscuits. Spring open the tin and slip the charlotte out. Whip the whipping or double cream, fill a piping bag and circle the top of the charlotte with piped rosettes. Place a mandarin segment on top of each rosette. Keep chilled until served.

Above: Charlotte Russe

Index